The Love We Make

Finding Fulfillment beyond Family Failures

Mona

Copyright © Mona 2024

All Rights Reserved

No part of this publication may be reproduced, distributed, or transmitted in any form or by any means, including photocopying, recording, or other electronic or mechanical methods, without the author's prior written permission, except in the case of brief quotations embodied in critical reviews and certain other non-commercial uses permitted by copyright law. For permission requests, please get in touch with the author.

- DEDICATION I
- ABOUT THE AUTHOR II
- INTRODUCTION A PRELUDE TO HEALING AND UNDERSTANDING 1
- CHAPTER 1 THE MANY FACES OF FAMILY 3
  - CHAPTER 1.2 THE EVOLUTION OF FAMILY: A HISTORICAL PERSPECTIVE 5
  - CHAPTER 1.3 RECOGNIZING DIVERSITY: SINGLE-PARENT, BLENDED, AND OTHER FORMS OF FAMILY UNITS 8
- CHAPTER 2 THE PILLARS OF FAMILY LIFE 16
  - CHAPTER 2.1 EXPLORING THE PURPOSE OF FAMILY STRUCTURES 22
  - CHAPTER 2.2 NURTURING IDENTITY AND VALUES WITHIN FAMILY DYNAMICS 26
- CHAPTER 3 THE SHADOWS OF NEGLECT: EFFECTS ON ATTACHMENT STYLES AND RELATIONSHIP ANXIETY 28
  - CHAPTER 3.1 FINANCIAL NEGLECT: THE IMPACT ON CHILD DEVELOPMENT 31
  - CHAPTER 3.2 EMOTIONAL ABSENCE: SCARS OF THE UNSEEN WOUNDS 35
  - CHAPTER 3.3 SPIRITUAL VOID: SEARCHING FOR MEANING AND BELONGING 43
- CHAPTER 4: THE JOURNEY TO INNER HEALING 45
  - CHAPTER 4.1 UNVEILING THE INNER CHILD: UNDERSTANDING ITS NEEDS AND WOUNDS 49
  - CHAPTER 4.2 THE TRAUMAS OF THE CAREGIVER: BREAKING THE CYCLE OF SUFFERING 51
- CHAPTER 5 RECOGNISING THE SIGNS: WHEN YOU'RE IN NEED OF HEALING .. 55
  - CHAPTER 5.1 IDENTIFYING THE ECHOES OF NEGLECT IN ADULT BEHAVIOR 62
  - CHAPTER 5.2 ACKNOWLEDGING THE PROBLEM: THE FIRST STEP TOWARDS HEALING 66
  - CHAPTER 5.3 SEEKING HELP: THERAPY AND SUPPORT NETWORKS 72
- CHAPTER 6 NURTURING YOUR INNER CHILD 76
  - CHAPTER 6.1 STRATEGIES FOR SELF-COMPASSION AND SELF-LOVE 80
  - CHAPTER 6.2 BUILDING HEALTHY RELATIONSHIPS: LEARNING TO TRUST AND LOVE AGAIN 83
  - CHAPTER 6.3 ESTABLISHING BOUNDARIES: PROTECTING YOUR EMOTIONAL WELL-BEING 86
- CHAPTER 7 FORGIVING AND MOVING FORWARD 89
  - CHAPTER 7.2 RECONCILING WITH THE PAST: UNDERSTANDING BUT NOT EXCUSING 93
  - CHAPTER 7.3 BUILDING A NEW LEGACY: THE CHOICE OF LOVE OVER RESENTMENT 96

Dedication

To My mum Sandra Downer, my strength and CLFM ministry Apostle Simmonds, Charles Rayson and my children Gabrielle Robinson Giovanni Martin Amayah Rayson.

About the Author

Ramona Rayson is an emerging voice in the literary world, hailed for her poignant narratives and heartfelt reflections on overcoming personal struggles. Born in Jamaica and raised in a quaint town nestled in the picturesque landscapes of Hertfordshire, England, Ramona, drawing from her own experience, embarked on a cathartic journey of self-discovery. Through her raw and honest prose, she invites readers into her world, offering glimpses of vulnerability and hope.

Introduction
A Prelude to Healing and Understanding

In the tapestry of human experience, there exists a spectrum of emotions and challenges that shape our lives in profound ways. Among these, few experiences carry the weight and complexity of not receiving love from a primary caregiver. Whether due to neglect, emotional unavailability, or outright abandonment, the absence of nurturing love in our formative years can leave indelible scars on our hearts and minds.

This prelude delves into the depths of this poignant topic, exploring the intricate layers of pain, longing, and resilience that accompany the journey of healing and understanding. It is a narrative of courage and vulnerability, of confronting the shadows of the past in order to embrace the light of self-discovery and acceptance.

A Prelude to Healing and Understanding

Throughout this exploration, we will navigate the labyrinth of emotions that arise from the absence of love from a primary caregiver, delving into the profound impact it can have on our sense of self-worth, our capacity for intimacy, and our ability to navigate the complexities of human relationships.

But amidst the darkness, there exists a glimmer of hope—a beacon of light that illuminates the path to healing and understanding. Through introspection, compassion, and a willingness to confront our deepest wounds, we can embark on a journey of transformation, turning pain into wisdom and brokenness into strength.

Together, let us embark on this prelude to healing and understanding, embracing the complexities of our shared human experience and discovering the resilience that lies within us all, for it is in the act of embracing our vulnerability that we find the courage to heal, and in the journey of understanding that we find the power to reclaim our lives and rewrite our stories.

Chapter 1
The Many Faces of Family

In the tapestry of human existence, the concept of family weaves itself into the very fabric of our being, shaping our identities and influencing the course of our lives in profound ways. For centuries, the notion of family has transcended cultural, social, and geographical boundaries, evolving to encompass a myriad of forms and configurations. Yet, at its core, the family remains a fundamental aspect of the human experience—a source of love, support, and belonging that fulfils our deepest emotional needs.

As Sarah navigated the complexities of her own familial dynamics, she couldn't help but ponder the myriad ways in which family manifested itself in the world around her. From the traditional nuclear family unit to the extended networks of kinship and community, the definition of family seemed to encompass a spectrum of relationships that defied easy categorization.

At its essence, Sarah understood family was more than just a biological bond—it was a sanctuary of love and acceptance, a refuge from the storms of life that provided solace and strength in times of need. It was a place where laughter echoed in the halls, and tears were met with comforting arms, where shared experiences forged connections that transcended the boundaries of blood and biology.

But for many, the concept of family extended far beyond the confines of biology, encompassing chosen families forged through friendship, shared values, and mutual support. These families, Sarah realized, were no less valid or meaningful than those bound by genetics, their bonds strengthened by the shared experiences and trials of life.

As Sarah contemplated the purpose of family, she came to understand that its significance lay not only in the fulfilment of our emotional needs but also in its role as a cornerstone of society—a nurturing environment where children learn the values of empathy, compassion, and cooperation that form the bedrock of a thriving community.

In a world marked by uncertainty and change, family provided a sense of stability and continuity—an anchor that grounded us in times of upheaval and uncertainty. It was a source of identity and belonging, a reminder that we were never truly alone in the vast expanse of the world.

But perhaps most importantly, the family offered us the opportunity to love and be loved—to share our joys and sorrows with those who knew us best and to celebrate the rich tapestry of human experience in all its complexity and diversity.

And so, as Sarah reflected on the many faces of the family that surrounded her, she felt a profound sense of gratitude for the bonds that held her close—a reminder that, no matter where life's journey took her, she would always have a place to call home.

Chapter 1.2

The Evolution of Family: A Historical Perspective

Throughout the annals of history, the concept of family has undergone a remarkable evolution, shaped by the shifting tides of culture, society, and ideology. From the earliest hunter-gatherer societies to the complex civilizations of the modern era, the structure and function of families have evolved in response to changing social, economic, and technological dynamics.

In ancient civilizations such as Mesopotamia and Egypt, families were often organized along patriarchal lines, with the eldest male serving as the head of the household and exercising authority over its members. These familial structures were tightly knit, with kinship ties extending across multiple generations and serving as the foundation of social order and stability.

As societies transitioned from agrarian to urban lifestyles, the dynamics of family life underwent significant changes. The rise of city-states and empires brought about new economic opportunities and social hierarchies, leading to the emergence of nuclear families as the primary unit of social organization. In these urban centres, families were often smaller and more mobile, with individuals migrating in search of work and economic opportunities.

The medieval period witnessed the influence of religious institutions on the concept of family, with marriage and procreation viewed as sacred duties ordained by God. The Church played a central role in regulating marital relationships and defining the rights and responsibilities of family members, shaping the moral and ethical framework within which families operated.

During the Renaissance and Enlightenment eras, the concept of family underwent further transformation as new philosophical and scientific ideas challenged traditional beliefs and practices. The rise of humanism and individualism led to greater emphasis on personal autonomy and freedom within familial relationships, with individuals seeking to carve out their own paths separate from the dictates of tradition and authority.

The Industrial Revolution brought about profound changes in the structure of families, as mass urbanization and industrialization led to the fragmentation of traditional familial bonds. With the rise of factory work and wage labour, families became increasingly nuclear in nature, with husbands and wives often working outside the home to support their households.

In the 20th century, the concept of family continued to evolve in response to shifting social norms and values. The rise of feminism and the civil rights movement challenged traditional gender roles and power dynamics within families, leading to greater equality and autonomy for women and marginalized groups. The legalization of same-sex marriage and advancements in reproductive technology further expanded the definition of family, recognizing the rights of LGBTQ+ individuals to form families of their own.

Today, the concept of family encompasses a diverse array of structures and relationships, reflecting the rich tapestry of human experience in the modern era. From traditional nuclear families to blended families, single-parent households, and chosen families, the definition of family continues to evolve in response to the needs and aspirations of individuals and communities.

Examples abound of this diverse landscape of family structures. In some cultures, extended families remain the norm, with multiple generations living together under one roof and sharing resources and responsibilities. In others, cohabiting couples or unmarried partners form the basis of familial units, challenging traditional notions of marriage and kinship.

Research from historians, anthropologists, and sociologists provides valuable insights into the historical evolution of family structures and dynamics. Studies have shown that familial arrangements vary widely across cultures and historical contexts, influenced by factors such as economic conditions, religious beliefs, and political systems.

For instance, research on medieval Europe reveals the importance of kinship ties and inheritance patterns in shaping familial relationships, with extended families playing a central role in agricultural societies. Similarly, studies of ancient civilizations such as Rome and Greece shed light on the role of patriarchal authority and gender dynamics within familial structures.

In summary, the evolution of family over time is a testament to the adaptive nature of human society as individuals and communities navigate the complexities of social, economic, and cultural change. By examining the historical roots of familial relationships and structures, we gain a deeper understanding of the diverse ways in which families have shaped and been shaped by the course of human history.

Chapter 1.3
Recognizing Diversity: Single-Parent, Blended, and Other Forms of Family Units

In the tapestry of human experience, the diversity of family structures and dynamics reflects the complexity and richness of the human condition. From single-parent households to blended families and other non-traditional arrangements, the myriad forms of family units offer a kaleidoscope of experiences and challenges that shape the lives of individuals and communities alike.

Consider the example of Maria, a single mother raising her two children on her own after the dissolution of her marriage. Despite the challenges she faces as the sole provider for her family, Maria takes pride in the strength and resilience she has cultivated in herself and her children. Through her unwavering love and determination, she demonstrates the power of single-parent families to thrive and flourish in the face of adversity.

Similarly, the story of David and Emily, a blended family formed through remarriage, highlights the complexities and joys of navigating relationships and dynamics within non-traditional family units. With children from previous marriages and a shared commitment to building a new life together, David and Emily exemplify the resilience and adaptability of blended families in forging bonds of love and unity across diverse backgrounds.

Beyond single-parent and blended families, the landscape of family diversity encompasses a multitude of other forms and configurations, including cohabiting couples, same-sex partnerships, and chosen families. Each of these arrangements offers unique opportunities and challenges, shaping the lived experiences of individuals and communities in profound ways.

The impact of family diversity extends beyond the confines of individual households, influencing broader social attitudes and policies surrounding issues such as marriage, parenting, and kinship. In recent years, there has been growing recognition of the need to embrace and celebrate the diversity of family structures, challenging traditional norms and stereotypes that may marginalize or stigmatize non-traditional families.

At the same time, however, diversity within family units can also present certain challenges and complexities. Single-parent households, for example, may face financial strain and time constraints as a result of the absence of a second income or co-parenting support. Blended families, on the other hand, may contend with issues related to child custody, sibling rivalries, and navigating relationships with ex-spouses.

Yet despite these challenges, there are also numerous advantages to be found in the diversity of family units. Single-parent households, for instance, may foster greater independence and resilience in children as they learn to navigate the world with the support of a strong and determined parent. Blended families, meanwhile, offer the opportunity for individuals to form new bonds and relationships, creating a sense of belonging and unity that transcends biological ties.

Ultimately, the recognition of diversity within family units serves as a testament to the resilience and adaptability of the human spirit. By embracing the myriad forms of family structures and dynamics that exist in the world, we honour the unique experiences and contributions of individuals and communities, fostering a more inclusive and compassionate society for all.

Impacts of an Absent Parent

An absent parent, whether due to divorce, separation, or other circumstances, can have profound and lasting effects on a child's emotional, spiritual, and financial well-being. Emotionally, children may experience feelings of abandonment, rejection, and low self-esteem as they grapple with the absence of a parent figure in their lives. Spiritually, the absence of parental guidance and support may leave children feeling adrift and disconnected from their sense of identity and purpose. Financially, single-parent households may face greater economic strain and instability as the burden of providing for the family falls on one individual.

Consider the case of Sarah, whose father left the family when she was just a young child. Despite her mother's best efforts to provide love and support, Sarah struggled with feelings of inadequacy and abandonment throughout her childhood. As she grew older, she found herself seeking validation and approval from others, longing for the love and acceptance she never received from her absent father.

Impacts of a Parent That Abandons Their Child

The abandonment of a child by a parent can have devastating effects on their emotional, spiritual, and financial well-being. Emotionally, children may experience feelings of betrayal, anger, and confusion as they grapple with the sudden loss of a parental figure. Spiritually, the absence of parental love and support may leave children feeling abandoned by those they trusted most, leading to a crisis of faith and identity.

Consider the story of Alex, whose mother abandoned him when he was just a baby, leaving him to be raised by his grandmother. Despite her love and devotion, Alex struggled with feelings of rejection and unworthiness throughout his childhood. As he grew older, he found himself longing for the love and acceptance he never received from his absent mother, searching for a sense of belonging and identity in the world.

Once upon a time, there was a bond between you and your mom that seemed unbreakable, woven with love, trust, and understanding. You shared secrets, dreams, and laughter, creating a world where you felt safe and cherished.

But as time passed, life presented challenges that strained your relationship. Misunderstandings arose, tensions flared, and one day, in a moment of heated disagreement, your mom uttered words that shattered your heart: "I can't do this anymore. You need to leave."

The pain of those words pierced your soul, leaving you feeling abandoned and lost. You couldn't comprehend how the one person who was supposed to protect you could cast you aside so easily. Betrayal and confusion engulfed you, leaving scars that seemed impossible to heal.

As you packed your belongings, each item held memories of happier times spent with your mom – the scent of her perfume on a scarf, the echo of her laughter in old photographs, the warmth of her embrace in a worn-out sweater. Each memento felt like a stab in the heart, a reminder of what you were losing.

Stepping out into the world alone, you felt a wave of vulnerability wash over you. The streets were unfamiliar, the night unforgiving, and the weight of rejection heavy on your shoulders. Tears blurred your vision as you navigated through the darkness, longing for the comfort of home, for the reassurance of your mom's love.

Days turned into weeks, and weeks turned into months, but the ache in your heart remained. You searched for solace in fleeting moments of distraction, in the kindness of strangers, in the whispers of forgotten dreams. Yet, no matter how hard you tried to numb the pain, it lingered like a shadow, a constant reminder of the void left by your mom's absence.

As a child, Sarah harboured deep resentment towards her mother. She perceived her mother as insensitive, selfish, and emotionally distant. Sarah felt that her mother lacked empathy and disregarded the feelings of others, including her own. This led to a profound lack of respect for her mother's authority and guidance.

Sarah's relationship with her mother was strained from a young age. She struggled to connect with her mother emotionally, feeling a sense of emptiness and longing for her mother's love and validation. Despite her efforts to seek her mother's affection, Sarah often found herself disappointed and unfulfilled.

Sarah's feelings of resentment and frustration towards her mother fueled a rebellious streak in her behaviour. She resisted her mother's attempts to impose rules and boundaries, viewing them as unjust and arbitrary. Sarah felt misunderstood and unsupported by her mother, further exacerbating their strained relationship.

From a young age, she felt like the odd one out in her family, never quite receiving the love and acceptance she yearned for. Her extended family's subtle acts of jealousy only added to her feelings of isolation.

As Sarah grew older, her search for love led her down a tumultuous path. Desperate to fill the void in her heart, she sought affection in the arms of men, hoping to find solace in their embrace. But each encounter left her feeling emptier than before, as she realized that the love she craved was elusive, slipping through her fingers like sand.

Despite the outward beauty that adorned her, Sarah's inner turmoil only deepened with each passing day. The attention she received from men only served to reinforce her belief that love was a fleeting illusion, a mirage in the desert of her existence.

Yet, beneath the layers of pain and disillusionment, a flicker of hope remained alive within Sarah's heart. A tiny ember of resilience, whispering that perhaps one day, she would find the love she so desperately sought. And so, with each sunrise, Sarah rose from the ashes of her past, determined to keep searching, to keep believing that somewhere out there, love truly existed, waiting to embrace her with open arms.

As Sarah grew older, she realized that her mother's behaviour stemmed from her own unresolved issues and struggles. She began to empathize with her mother's experiences and recognise the complexity of their relationship dynamics. Although forgiveness and reconciliation were challenging, Sarah embarked on a journey towards healing and understanding.

Through therapy and self-reflection, Sarah confronted her feelings of anger and resentment towards her mother. She learned to set boundaries and prioritize her own emotional well-being, even in the face of familial expectations. Despite the lingering wounds from her childhood, Sarah gradually found peace and acceptance within herself.

Impacts on Child Development

The absence or abandonment of a parent can have profound effects on a child's development, influencing their emotional, social, and cognitive growth in significant ways. Research has shown that children raised in single-parent households or by caregivers other than their biological parents may be at greater risk for emotional and behavioural problems, including depression, anxiety, and conduct disorders. They may also struggle with issues related to attachment and trust, as well as difficulties forming healthy relationships with others.

In contrast, children raised in stable and supportive family environments, whether traditional nuclear families or alternative arrangements such as blended families or chosen families, tend to fare better in terms of their overall well-being and development. They may benefit from positive role models and consistent parental support, as well as a sense of security and belonging within the family unit.

Consider the example of Mia, who was raised by her grandparents after her parents passed away in a tragic accident. Despite the loss she experienced at a young age, Mia thrived in her grandparents' loving and nurturing care, growing into a resilient and compassionate young woman. With their guidance and support, she was able to overcome the challenges she faced and build a bright future for herself.

In conclusion, the absence or abandonment of a parent can have profound and lasting effects on a child's emotional, spiritual, and financial well-being. It is crucial for parents, caregivers, and society as a whole to recognise the importance of providing love, support, and stability to children, regardless of their family structure or circumstances. By investing in the well-being of our children, we can help them grow into happy, healthy, and resilient individuals capable of reaching their full potential.

Chapter 2
The Pillars of Family Life

In the intricate tapestry of family life, there often emerges a figure who stands as the unwavering pillar upon which the entire family relies—a source of strength, wisdom, and guidance that sustains and nurtures all who are fortunate enough to be under their care.

Consider the story of James, a devoted father who works tirelessly to provide for his family and create a nurturing home environment for his children. Despite the challenges he faces in balancing work and family responsibilities, James remains steadfast in his commitment to being a pillar of support for his loved ones. Whether it's offering words of encouragement during difficult times or providing a listening ear when his children need someone to talk to, James exemplifies the qualities of a true family pillar, demonstrating selflessness, compassion, and resilience in the face of adversity.

Similarly, there is Maria, a grandmother who has taken on the role of primary caregiver for her grandchildren after the untimely passing of their parents. Despite her own grief and loss, Maria rises to the occasion with grace and strength, providing a stable and loving home environment where her grandchildren can heal and thrive. Through her unwavering love and devotion, Maria serves as a beacon of hope and stability in the midst of tragedy, embodying the qualities of a true family pillar in every sense of the word.

But how do we know who the pillar of the family is? It is not always evident at first glance, for the role of the pillar is not determined by age, gender, or social status but by the depth of their commitment and the strength of their character. The pillar of the family is the one who leads by example, who demonstrates resilience in the face of adversity, and who embodies the values and principles upon which the family is built.

Their role extends far beyond mere physical presence; they are the emotional anchor that keeps the family grounded in times of turmoil, the voice of reason that provides clarity amidst chaos and the nurturing spirit that fosters growth and healing within the family unit.

But perhaps most importantly, the pillar of the family is entrusted with the sacred responsibility of creating a safe and nurturing environment in which children can thrive. This means not only providing for their physical needs but also attending to their emotional well-being, fostering a sense of security and belonging, and instilling values of empathy, compassion, and emotional intelligence.

Teaching emotional intelligence is essential in ensuring that the family environment is conducive to healthy development. This involves helping children recognise and understand their own emotions, as well as those of others, and teaching them constructive ways of expressing and managing their feelings. By cultivating empathy, resilience, and self-awareness, we empower children to navigate life's challenges with grace and confidence, laying the foundation for a lifetime of emotional well-being and fulfilment.

Being a pillar of the family can be both a privilege and a burden. As parents, we often bear the weight of responsibility on our shoulders, striving to provide for our children's needs while navigating the complexities of daily life. However, amidst the hustle and bustle, it's easy to overlook the profound impact our actions and behaviours can have on our children.

Many times, we operate on autopilot, unaware of how our words, attitudes, and actions shape our children's perceptions of themselves and the world around them. We may unintentionally pass down patterns of behaviour that we ourselves inherited from our own upbringing, perpetuating cycles of dysfunction without even realising it.

It's essential to recognise that our children are sponges, soaking up every interaction, every expression, and every nuance of our behaviour. When we are not conscious of our actions, we risk inflicting wounds that may go unnoticed until it's too late.

In writing this book, my intention is not to condemn or criticize but rather to encourage self-reflection and growth. By acknowledging the potential impact of our behaviours on our children, we empower ourselves to make positive changes that foster their development and well-being.

As parents, we must strive to be mindful of our words and actions, recognizing that even the smallest gestures can leave a lasting impression. It's not about being perfect but rather about being aware and willing to learn and grow alongside our children.

Together, let us embark on a journey of self-discovery and transformation, committing to do better and be better for the sake of our children's futures. With compassion, understanding, and a willingness to change, we can create a nurturing environment where our children can thrive and flourish. Listen to Sarah's story that we are all guilty of.

Sarah sat alone in her dimly lit living room, lost in thought. She had just finished reading a chapter of a parenting book she picked up at the local bookstore, and its words had struck a chord deep within her.

Sarah was a devoted mother to two young children, Emily and Jacob. She worked tirelessly to provide for their needs, juggling the demands of her job and household responsibilities with grace and determination. Yet, as she reflected on the book's message, she couldn't shake the nagging feeling that she might be missing something crucial in her parenting journey.

As if on cue, Emily, her eldest, padded into the room, her small frame dwarfed by the oversized book clutched in her hands. "Mommy, can you read me a story?" she asked, her voice tinged with innocence and hope.

Sarah smiled, her heart swelling with love for her daughter. "Of course, sweetheart," she replied, patting the space beside her on the couch. As Emily settled in beside her, Sarah began to read, the words flowing effortlessly from her lips.

But as she read, Sarah couldn't help but notice a pang of guilt gnawing at her conscience. She recalled moments when she had snapped at Emily in frustration or when she had been too preoccupied with work to truly listen to her daughter's stories. She realized that, despite her best intentions, she had allowed the pressures of daily life to overshadow the importance of being present for her children.

Tears welled up in Sarah's eyes as she reached the end of the story, the weight of her realization pressing down on her chest like a leaden weight. She knew she needed to make a change, to become more conscious of her behaviours and their impact on her children.

With a newfound resolve, Sarah made a silent vow to herself and her children. She pledged to be more mindful, more present, and more attuned to their needs. She knew it wouldn't be easy, but she was willing to try for the sake of her children's happiness and well-being.

As she tucked Emily into bed later that evening, Sarah whispered a promise into her daughter's ear. "I love you more than words can say, Emily. And I promise to do everything in my power to be the best mommy I can be."

And as Emily drifted off to sleep, a smile graced her lips, a silent affirmation of the bond between mother and child and the enduring power of love and growth.

In conclusion, the pillar of the family is a cornerstone of strength and stability, providing love, support, and guidance to all its members. By recognizing the importance of this role and nurturing its development within our own families, we can create environments that are safe, nurturing, and conducive to the healthy growth and development of children. Through the teaching of emotional intelligence and the cultivation of empathy and resilience, we can ensure that our families remain strong and resilient in the face of life's challenges, laying the groundwork for a future filled with love, harmony, and fulfilment.

Chapter 2.1
Exploring the Purpose of Family Structures

As a Jamaican navigating life in the UK, the journey of adapting to a new cultural landscape brings to light the profound influence of family structures on individual development. For individuals like Jamal, the shift from the cultural norms and values of Jamaica to those of the UK underscores the significance of family in shaping one's identity and worldview.

Jamal's experience highlights the importance of understanding the purpose of family structures within different cultural contexts. In Jamaica, family is often not seen as the cornerstone of society, with strong emphasis placed on collective responsibility, respect for elders, and interconnectedness within the community. From an early age, Jamal was instilled with these values, learning the importance of family bonds and the role they play in shaping individual identity and belonging.

However, upon relocating to the UK, Jamal found himself navigating a cultural landscape that differed significantly from his upbringing in Jamaica. Here, family structures may take on different forms and priorities, with greater emphasis placed on individualism, personal autonomy, and diversity of family arrangements. Jamal's journey of adaptation required him to reconcile the values and expectations of his Jamaican heritage with those of his new environment, navigating the complexities of cultural change while staying true to his roots.

The impact of this cultural transition on Jamal's development cannot be overstated. From navigating differences in communication styles and social norms to grappling with new moral and ethical values, Jamal's journey underscores the transformative power of family structures in shaping individual identity and resilience.

In the UK, Jamal found himself exposed to a diverse array of perspectives and experiences, challenging him to broaden his understanding of the world and adapt to new ways of thinking and living. Through it all, his family remained a constant source of support and guidance, offering him a sense of stability and belonging amidst the uncertainties of cultural change.

Ultimately, Jamal's journey highlights the dynamic interplay between culture and family structures in shaping individual development. Across different cultural contexts, families serve as the primary agents of socialization, transmitting values, beliefs, and traditions from one generation to the next. By navigating the complexities of cultural change while staying grounded in the values of his Jamaican heritage, Jamal demonstrates the resilience and adaptability that come from a strong foundation of family support and connection.

The dynamics of parenting in Caribbean cultures, including Jamaica, often carry a heavy emphasis on discipline and respect. Many of us grew up in environments where the fear of disappointing or embarrassing our parents loomed large, knowing that disobedience could result in physical punishment. However, as we reflect on our own experiences and observe the world around us, we come to realize that the cycle of fear and punishment is not the answer.

Smacking, or any form of physical punishment, can indeed have lasting negative effects on children, causing trauma and eroding their sense of security and self-worth. Instead, what our children truly need is love, understanding, and guidance. It's essential to break away from the old patterns of harsh discipline and embrace more compassionate and nurturing approaches to parenting.

Yet, despite our understanding of the harm inflicted by abandonment and disrespect, we still see a troubling trend of men abandoning their responsibilities as fathers. Many of these men, having themselves experienced abandonment or neglect, perpetuate the cycle by walking away from their children and the mothers who care for them. In doing so, they heap additional burdens onto the shoulders of already struggling mothers, perpetuating a cycle of pain and dysfunction.

As someone who has grappled with these challenges firsthand, I understand the complexities involved. But I also recognise the importance of breaking free from these destructive patterns and taking responsibility for our actions. It's time for us to challenge the notion of strength equating to emotional detachment and instead embrace the courage it takes to show love, to be present, and to support our children and their mothers.

Love is indeed the solution. It's the foundation upon which healthy families are built, and it's the key to breaking free from the cycle of abandonment and neglect. By choosing love over fear, by choosing compassion over punishment, we can create a brighter future for our children and ourselves. It's time to break the cycle and pave the way for healing and growth, one loving and supportive relationship at a time.

In conclusion, the purpose of family structures extends beyond geographical boundaries, transcending cultural differences to shape individual identity and development. For individuals like Jamal, navigating life in a new cultural context requires a delicate balance of embracing new experiences while staying grounded in the values and traditions of the family. Through it all, the family remains the steadfast pillar upon which individuals can rely, offering love, support, and guidance as they navigate the complexities of cultural change and personal growth.

Chapter 2.2

Nurturing Identity and Values within Family Dynamics

In the delicate tapestry of family dynamics, mothers and fathers serve as the guiding lights, shaping the identity and values of their children through their love, guidance, and example. Each parent plays a unique and irreplaceable role in the development of their offspring, contributing to their growth and well-being in profound ways. However, the journey of parenthood is not without its trials and tribulations, as real-life experiences often underscore the complexities and challenges faced by individuals striving to uphold their roles as mothers and fathers.

As a Jamaican woman navigating life in the UK, I, too, have experienced firsthand the highs and lows of motherhood and the impact of absent fathers on family dynamics. When I had my third child, a daughter, her father made the heart-wrenching decision to abandon us, leaving me to navigate the complexities of single parenthood while grappling with feelings of betrayal and abandonment. The emotional toll of this experience was immense as I struggled to come to terms with the reality of raising three children alone.

Psychologically, I battled with feelings of worthlessness and self-doubt, questioning my ability to provide for my children's emotional and material needs. Yet, in the midst of my darkest moments, I found solace in my unwavering love for my children, drawing strength from the bond we shared and the determination to create a better future for them.

The financial strain of single parenthood only added to my burden, as I worked tirelessly to make ends meet while juggling the demands of work and childcare. Yet, despite the challenges, I remained steadfast in my commitment to providing my children with love, stability, and a sense of belonging.

In my journey of healing and self-discovery, I sought solace in pursuing studies in counselling, seeking to understand and navigate the complexities of my own emotions while offering support to others facing similar struggles. Through this process, I learned to let go of the shame and stigma surrounding my circumstances, embracing my identity as a strong and capable mother despite the absence of a father figure in my children's lives.

As I reflect on my experiences and the cultural dynamics that shape my identity as a Jamaican woman, I am struck by the resilience and strength of my fellow countrymen and women, who navigate the complexities of family life with grace and fortitude. It is this resilience that inspires me to share my story, breaking the silence surrounding single parenthood and challenging the stereotypes and judgments that often accompany it.

In conclusion, the journey of nurturing identity and values within family dynamics is a deeply personal and transformative one, marked by moments of growth, resilience, and love. As a mother, I have learned to embrace the challenges and triumphs of parenthood, drawing strength from the love and support of my children and the unwavering determination to create a brighter future for us all despite the obstacles we may face along the way.

Chapter 3
The Shadows of Neglect: Effects on Attachment Styles And Relationship Anxiety

As we delve into the depths of family dynamics, it becomes evident that neglect casts a long shadow, leaving lasting imprints on the emotional and psychological well-being of individuals. From infancy to adulthood, the effects of neglect can manifest in various attachment styles, shaping the way we perceive and navigate relationships with others.

Attachment theory posits that our early experiences with caregivers influence the development of attachment styles, which in turn shape our relationships throughout life. Secure attachment, characterised by a sense of trust, comfort, and security in relationships, is fostered by responsive and nurturing caregiving. However, neglectful or inconsistent caregiving can give rise to insecure attachment styles, including anxious and avoidant attachment.

For children who experience neglect, the absence of consistent and responsive caregiving can erode their sense of security and trust in relationships, leading to anxious attachment. These individuals may exhibit clingy or dependent behaviour in relationships, fearing abandonment and seeking constant reassurance from others.

Conversely, some individuals may develop avoidant attachment as a coping mechanism in response to neglect. These individuals may distance themselves emotionally from others, fearing vulnerability and intimacy as a result of past experiences of neglect.

My own journey through the shadows of neglect began in childhood, as I felt unseen and unheard within my own family. The absence of nurturing and supportive caregiving left me feeling adrift and disconnected, yearning for love and acceptance that seemed perpetually out of reach.

As a teenager, I found myself cast out of the family home, left to navigate the world on my own without the guidance and support of caregivers. The experience of abandonment and neglect during this formative period of my life left deep scars, shaping my perceptions of myself and others in profound ways.

Throughout my journey into adulthood, the effects of neglect continued to reverberate through my relationships, manifesting in feelings of anxiety and insecurity. I found myself oscillating between anxious and avoidant attachment patterns, struggling to trust others and form meaningful connections.

Yet, amidst the shadows of neglect, there is also hope and healing. Through therapy and self-reflection, I embarked on a journey of self-discovery and healing, confronting the wounds of the past and reclaiming my sense of worth and belonging. I learned to recognise the patterns of anxious and avoidant attachment within myself and to cultivate a more secure and resilient sense of self.

Today, as I navigate the complexities of relationships, I carry with me the lessons learned from my journey through neglect. I strive to create healthy boundaries, communicate openly and honestly with others, and cultivate a sense of compassion and empathy for myself and those around me.

In sharing my healing journey, I hope to shed light on the profound impact of neglect on attachment styles and relationship dynamics. By acknowledging the shadows of neglect and embracing the journey of healing and growth, we can reclaim our sense of agency and forge deeper, more meaningful connections with others.

Chapter 3.1

Financial Neglect: The Impact on Child Development

Growing up in a Jamaican household, financial struggles were often a familiar companion, shaping the landscape of my childhood and leaving lasting imprints on my development. The pressure to provide for a family amidst limited resources and economic hardships is a reality faced by many parents, and its impact on child development cannot be overstated.

Financial neglect, characterised by the inability or unwillingness of caregivers to adequately provide for the material needs of their children, casts a long shadow over the lives of young ones. From the absence of basic necessities such as food, clothing, and shelter to the inability to access educational opportunities and extracurricular activities, financial neglect can create barriers that hinder a child's growth and potential.

In a Jamaican household like mine, where financial resources were often scarce, the pressures of providing for a family weighed heavily on my parents. Despite their best efforts, there were times when we went without, when the stress of making ends meet overshadowed the joys of childhood.

The impact of financial neglect on child development extends beyond the realm of material deprivation, shaping the emotional and psychological well-being of young ones. The constant stress and anxiety surrounding financial instability can create a tense and uncertain environment in which children may struggle to feel safe and secure. Feelings of shame, inadequacy, and resentment may also arise as children internalise the messages of scarcity and lack.

Moreover, the cycle of financial neglect can perpetuate intergenerational poverty, as children growing up in financially disadvantaged households may face barriers to accessing higher education and career opportunities, perpetuating a cycle of economic hardship for generations to come.

Yet, amidst the challenges of financial neglect, there is also resilience and strength. From a young age, I learned the value of resourcefulness, creativity, and perseverance in the face of adversity. My parents instilled in me a strong work ethic and a sense of resilience that has served me well throughout my life.

Today, as I reflect on my upbringing and the impact of financial neglect on my development, I am reminded of the importance of breaking the cycle of poverty and providing opportunities for all children to thrive. By addressing the root causes of financial neglect and investing in programs and policies that support families in need, we can create a more equitable and just society in which every child has the opportunity to reach their full potential.

In the bustling streets of Kingston, Jamaica, lived a family of four: the Smiths. James, the father, worked long hours as a taxi driver, while Sarah, the mother, managed their small grocery store. Despite their hard work, making ends meet was a constant struggle.

As the eldest of two siblings, young Marcus often bore witness to the stress that permeated their household. Money was always tight, and conversations about bills and debts filled the air more often than laughter or joy. Yet, despite their financial woes, the

Smiths did their best to shield their children from the harsh realities of their situation.

However, as Marcus grew older, he couldn't help but notice the strain that money troubles placed on his parents' relationship. Arguments about finances became more frequent, and the tension in the household seemed to escalate with each passing day. Despite their best efforts, the weight of financial neglect began to take its toll on the family.

Marcus watched as his parents struggled to provide the basic necessities, often going without meals themselves to ensure that their children were fed. He witnessed the stress etched into their faces, the exhaustion evident in their weary eyes. And as much as he tried to hide his own worries, Marcus couldn't shake the feeling of uncertainty that gnawed at him day and night.

As the years went by, the financial strain only seemed to worsen. Marcus watched as his dreams of attending university faded into the distance, replaced by the stark reality of needing to find a job to help support his family. He felt the weight of responsibility bearing down on him, knowing that his parents were counting on him to ease their burden.

But amidst the struggle to make ends meet, Marcus couldn't help but feel a sense of resentment growing within him. He resented the fact that his parents had been unable to provide him with the opportunities he so desperately craved. He resented the sacrifices they had made on his behalf, knowing that they had come at great personal cost.

And as Marcus ventured out into the world, he carried with him the scars of financial neglect – scars that ran deep and left a lasting imprint on his psyche. He vowed to break free from the cycle of poverty that had ensnared his family, determined to carve out a better future for himself and the generations that would follow.

But as he embarked on his journey, Marcus couldn't help but wonder how different things might have been if only his parents had been given the support and resources they so desperately needed. He knew that financial neglect had robbed him of opportunities and dreams, leaving him to navigate a world that seemed determined to keep him down.

And as he looked back on his childhood, Marcus made a solemn promise to himself – that he would do everything in his power to ensure that no child would ever have to experience the pain and hardship of financial neglect again. For he knew that the scars it left behind were far too deep to ever truly heal.

In conclusion, financial neglect casts a long shadow over the lives of children, shaping their development in profound ways. From the pressures of providing for a family to the emotional and psychological toll of economic instability, the impact of financial neglect is far-reaching and enduring. Yet, amidst the challenges, there is also resilience and strength as children learn to navigate the complexities of poverty with grace and determination. By addressing the root causes of financial neglect and investing in the well-being of families, we can create a brighter future for all children, regardless of their socioeconomic background.

Chapter 3.2

Emotional Absence: Scars of the Unseen Wounds

In the intricate tapestry of human relationships, emotional absence casts a shadow that often goes unnoticed yet leaves deep wounds that can impact our lives in profound ways. Rooted in experiences of neglect, abandonment, or trauma, emotional absence manifests as a disconnection from our own feelings and those of others, leading to a sense of emptiness and longing that echoes through our lives.

For many of us, emotional absence begins in childhood, when we may have experienced neglect or emotional unavailability from caregivers. Growing up in environments where our emotional needs were not met, we learned to bury our feelings deep within ourselves, hiding them away in the recesses of our subconscious. Over time, this pattern of emotional suppression becomes ingrained, shaping the way we perceive and interact with the world around us.

As adults, we may find ourselves triggered by situations or relationships that mirror the feelings of abandonment or neglect we experienced in childhood. These triggers can evoke intense emotional responses, ranging from anxiety and fear to anger and sadness, as we grapple with the unresolved wounds of the past.

In our efforts to cope with the pain of emotional absence, some of us may turn to maladaptive coping mechanisms such as promiscuity. Seeking validation and connection through physical intimacy, we may engage in a cycle of fleeting relationships, searching for the love and acceptance we never received in our formative years. Yet, despite our efforts to fill the void, the emptiness remains, leaving us feeling more disconnected and alone than ever before.

To heal from the scars of emotional absence, we must first acknowledge and accept the pain that lies buried within us. This requires a willingness to confront the traumas of our past and the ways in which they continue to shape our lives in the present. By shining a light on the hidden wounds of emotional neglect, we can begin to reclaim our sense of self and reconnect with our emotions in a healthy and authentic way.

Healing from emotional absence also requires us to cultivate self-awareness and mindfulness, allowing ourselves to fully experience and express our feelings without judgment or shame. Through practices such as therapy, meditation, and journaling, we can learn to recognise and process our emotions in a constructive manner, paving the way for deeper healing and growth.

Moreover, we must recognise the impact of emotional absence on our attachment styles and relationships; for those of us who grew up without experiencing unconditional love and support, forming secure attachments can be challenging. We may struggle with feelings of unworthiness or fear of abandonment, leading to patterns of anxious or avoidant attachment in our relationships.

By acknowledging the scars of emotional absence and committing to our own healing journey, we can break free from the cycle of neglect and reclaim our sense of worth and belonging. Through self-reflection, self-care, and compassion for ourselves and others, we can begin to build healthier, more fulfilling relationships grounded in authenticity and connection. It is only by confronting the shadows of our past that we can truly step into the light of our own healing and transformation.

Loneliness is a deeply human experience that can profoundly affect our well-being and sense of belonging. It is a state of emotional isolation and disconnection, often characterised by feelings of emptiness, sadness, and longing for companionship. While loneliness can stem from various sources, one significant factor is the lack of love and nurturing from primary caregivers during childhood.

When a child does not receive love, care, and emotional support from their primary caregiver, it can have far-reaching consequences that extend into adulthood. The bond between a child and their caregiver lays the foundation for healthy emotional development, self-esteem, and the ability to form secure attachments with others. When this bond is absent or disrupted, it can leave a lasting imprint on the child's psyche, contributing to feelings of loneliness and inadequacy.

Children who grow up without the love and support of their primary caregiver may struggle to form secure attachments with others later in life. They may find it challenging to trust and open up to others, fearing rejection or abandonment. This can lead to a cycle of loneliness and isolation as they struggle to connect with others on a deep emotional level.

Furthermore, the absence of love from a primary caregiver can impact a child's sense of self-worth and identity. Children internalise the messages they receive from their caregivers, and when those messages are ones of neglect or indifference, it can lead to feelings of unworthiness and low self-esteem. These feelings may persist into adulthood, influencing how individuals perceive themselves and their place in the world.

Moreover, the lack of love and nurturing during childhood can affect one's ability to regulate emotions and cope with stress effectively. Without the support of a caring adult, children may struggle to develop healthy coping mechanisms, leading to difficulties managing emotions such as sadness, anger, or anxiety. This can contribute to feelings of loneliness and isolation, as individuals may feel unable to reach out for support or express their needs to others.

In a quaint village nestled among rolling hills and lush greenery lived a family of three: the Carters. John and Mary Carter were once deeply in love, their bond strong and unbreakable. But as the years passed, life's challenges took their toll, and the warmth that once filled their home began to fade.

John, a hardworking accountant, spent long hours at the office, buried beneath a mountain of paperwork and deadlines. Mary, a devoted homemaker, poured her heart and soul into caring for their young daughter, Lily. Yet, despite their physical presence, there was an emotional absence that lingered between them like a shadow.

As Lily grew older, she couldn't help but notice the growing divide between her parents. Their conversations became stilted and superficial, their laughter forced and hollow. It was as if they were merely going through the motions, their hearts a million miles away.

Despite their best efforts to shield her from their marital woes, Lily could sense the tension that hung heavy in the air. She watched as her parents drifted further and further apart, their love fading into the background like a forgotten melody.

With each passing day, Lily longed for the warmth and affection that seemed to elude her. She yearned for the sound of her parents' laughter, for the embrace of their love. But no matter how hard she tried, she couldn't bridge the gap that separated them.

And so, Lily learned to navigate the world on her own, seeking solace in the pages of books and the gentle whispers of nature. She found comfort in the company of friends and the warmth of community, forging her own path in a world filled with emotional absence.

As she grew into a young woman, Lily carried with her the scars of her parents' disconnection – scars that ran deep and left a lasting imprint on her soul. She vowed to break free from the cycle of emotional absence that had plagued her family for generations, determined to create a future filled with love, warmth, and connection.

And as she looked back on her childhood, Lily made a solemn promise to herself – that she would never allow the flame of love to flicker and fade but would nurture it with care and devotion, ensuring that it burned bright for all eternity, for she knew that true happiness could only be found in the embrace of love, in all its forms.

In essence, the absence of love from a primary caregiver can have profound and long-lasting effects on a person's emotional well-being and sense of connection with others. It is essential for individuals who have experienced this type of neglect to seek support and healing to address the wounds of their past and cultivate healthy relationships in the present. Through therapy, self-reflection, and self-care practices, it is possible to heal from the pain of childhood neglect and forge deeper connections with oneself and others.

When a child receives love and nurturing from their primary caregiver, it sets the stage for healthy emotional development and a positive relationship with food. The bond between a child and their caregiver forms the foundation for how the child perceives themselves, their needs, and their environment, including their relationship with food. Here's how receiving love from a primary caregiver can influence one's relationship with food:

Sense of Security and Trust: When a child feels loved and securely attached to their caregiver, they develop a sense of trust in the world around them. This feeling of security extends to their relationship with food, as they learn to trust their caregiver to provide nourishment and meet their basic needs. This trust forms the basis for a healthy relationship with food, where the child feels confident in their ability to listen to their body's hunger and fullness cues without fear or anxiety.

Emotional Regulation: Love and nurturing from a primary caregiver help children develop healthy emotional regulation skills. When children feel loved and supported, they learn to use food as a source of comfort and nourishment rather than as a coping mechanism for dealing with stress or negative emotions. They develop the ability to recognise and express their feelings in healthy ways rather than turning to food for emotional soothing.

Positive Body Image: Children who receive love and acceptance from their caregivers are more likely to develop a positive body image and self-esteem. They learn to appreciate their bodies for what they can do rather than focusing solely on appearance or weight. This positive self-image extends to their relationship with food, as they view eating as a way to nourish and care for their bodies rather than as a means of controlling their weight or appearance.

Healthy Eating Habits: Love and nurturing from a primary caregiver lay the groundwork for establishing healthy eating habits early in life. Children learn to enjoy a variety of foods and to eat intuitively, paying attention to their body's hunger and fullness signals. They are less likely to develop disordered eating patterns or engage in restrictive dieting behaviours, as they trust their body's innate wisdom to guide their food choices.

Family Mealtime Dynamics: Love and nurturing from a primary caregiver often translate into positive family mealtime dynamics. Children who feel loved and valued by their caregiver are more likely to have positive interactions with family members during mealtime, fostering a sense of connection and belonging. Family meals become a time for bonding and sharing rather than a source of tension or conflict.

Overall, receiving love and nurturing from a primary caregiver sets the stage for a healthy relationship with food based on trust, emotional regulation, positive body image, and intuitive eating habits. It lays the foundation for a lifetime of nourishment, enjoyment, and well-being around food.

Chapter 3.3

Spiritual Void: Searching for Meaning and Belonging

In the depths of emotional neglect and abandonment, a spiritual void often emerges—a yearning for meaning, purpose, and belonging that echoes through the corridors of our souls. Rooted in the absence of love and nurturing from our primary caregivers, this void leaves us feeling adrift and disconnected, searching for solace and fulfilment in a world that often feels cold and indifferent.

The biblical proverb, "The fathers have eaten sour grapes, and the children's teeth are set on edge," captures the intergenerational impact of our decisions and actions on future generations. As we grapple with the scars of our own upbringing, we must also confront the ripple effects that our choices have on our children and their emotional well-being.

For many of us, the search for meaning and belonging leads us down various paths as we seek love and validation from sources outside of ourselves. Some may turn to fleeting relationships or material possessions in an attempt to fill the void, only to find that true fulfilment remains elusive.

However, for others, the journey of healing and self-discovery leads us to seek solace in spiritual enlightenment. Through the exploration of faith and the teachings of scripture, we find a source of comfort and guidance that transcends the limitations of the physical world.

During my own journey of healing, I found solace and support in the embrace of a church community. Through the power of prayer, fellowship, and worship, I discovered a sense of belonging and purpose that had long eluded me. The teachings of scripture offered a roadmap for self-improvement and personal growth, inspiring me to strive for higher ideals and values.

The concept of "dying daily," as expressed in the Bible, became a guiding principle in my quest for spiritual enlightenment. It reminded me of the importance of continual self-examination and renewal as I sought to overcome the limitations of my flesh and align myself with higher spiritual truths.

Through my involvement in the church, I found the strength and resilience to confront the wounds of my past and embrace the journey of healing and transformation. The love and support of my spiritual community provided a safe space for me to explore my faith and cultivate a deeper connection with the divine.

As I continue on my spiritual journey, I am reminded of the profound impact that faith and spirituality can have on our lives. By seeking spiritual enlightenment, we can rise above the limitations of our earthly existence and tap into a source of infinite love and wisdom. Through the power of faith, we can heal the wounds of our past, empower ourselves to create a brighter future, and find true fulfilment and belonging in the embrace of the divine.

Chapter 4:
The Journey to Inner Healing

In the journey of life, there comes a time when we must confront the wounds of our past and embark on a path of inner healing. Rooted in the recognition of our own pain and the desire to break free from its grip, this journey is a transformative process of forgiveness, self-discovery, and self-love.

At a particular age, we may have experienced trauma or neglect that left deep scars on our psyche, shaping the way we perceive ourselves and the world around us. Whether it was the absence of love and nurturing from our caregivers or the pain of abandonment and rejection, these wounds continue to linger within us, affecting our thoughts, feelings, and behaviours.

In order to heal from these wounds, we must first acknowledge and accept the pain that lies buried within us. This requires a willingness to confront the traumas of our past and the ways in which they continue to influence our lives in the present. By shining a light on the hidden wounds of our childhood, we can begin to release the hold they have over us and reclaim our sense of self-worth and dignity.

Forgiveness plays a central role in the journey to inner healing. It is not about excusing the actions of those who hurt us or denying the pain they caused, but rather about freeing ourselves from the burden of resentment and anger that weighs us down. By extending forgiveness to ourselves and others, we open the door to healing and transformation, allowing love and compassion to flow freely into our lives.

As part of this process, it is important to give love and support to the wounded child within us. This means nurturing ourselves with kindness and compassion and offering ourselves the love and acceptance we may have longed for but never received. By reconnecting with the innocence and vulnerability of our inner child, we can begin to heal the wounds of our past and cultivate a deeper sense of self-love and acceptance.

Through practices such as therapy, journaling, and meditation, we can create a safe space for our inner child to express their pain and receive the healing they so desperately need. By listening to their cries and offering them comfort and reassurance, we can begin to mend the broken pieces of our souls and reclaim our sense of wholeness and well-being.

As we journey towards inner healing, we must remember that it is a process, not a destination. It requires patience, perseverance, and self-compassion as we navigate the twists and turns of our inner landscape. But with each step we take, we move closer to the freedom and joy that comes from releasing the past and embracing the present moment with an open heart and a renewed sense of purpose.

As humans, we often find ourselves grappling with situations that we wish were different. We resist what is, clinging to the hope that things will miraculously change on their own. However, it is in this resistance that we inadvertently create more suffering for ourselves. The implications of not accepting "what is" are profound, leading to a perpetual cycle of struggle and discontent.

When we refuse to accept our life situations, we resist the flow of life and block the natural energy of change. Our circumstances remain stagnant, and we find ourselves trapped in a state of frustration and despair. It's like trying to swim against the current of a powerful river—you exhaust yourself, but you never make any progress.

But once we are able to surrender and accept "what is," a remarkable shift occurs. Acceptance is not resignation or defeat; it is an acknowledgement of reality and a willingness to work with it rather than against it. When we accept our life situations, we open ourselves up to a new level of power and agency. We no longer waste our energy fighting against the inevitable; instead, we channel it into creating positive change.

Acceptance allows us to release resistance and embrace the present moment fully. It is a profound act of surrender, a letting go of the need to control or manipulate our circumstances. And in that surrender, we find peace and liberation.

Moreover, acceptance creates space for new possibilities to emerge. When we stop resisting and start accepting, we invite a new energy into our lives—a creative force that can transform even the most challenging situations. It is like opening a door that was once closed, allowing fresh air and light to flood in.

Challenges and struggles are not meant to break us; they are invitations to spiritual growth and transformation. Each obstacle we face is an opportunity to deepen our understanding of ourselves and the world around us. It is in facing adversity that we uncover our inner strength and resilience and emerge stronger and wiser than before.

In relationships, too, acceptance plays a crucial role. When we find ourselves in constant conflict with our partners, it is often a reflection of our own unresolved issues and insecurities. Instead of blaming or criticising our partners, we can use these challenges as opportunities for self-reflection and growth. By accepting our own flaws and limitations, we create space for greater harmony and connection in our relationships.

For me, the journey of acceptance was transformative. I spent years trapped in a victim mindset, blaming others for my struggles and feeling powerless to change my circumstances. But as I learned to accept "what is" and take responsibility for my own life, I discovered a newfound sense of empowerment and freedom.

Yes, challenges will arise, and there will be moments of doubt and uncertainty. But as long as we are willing to face them with courage and humility, they can become stepping stones to greater spiritual enlightenment and personal growth. So, let us embrace acceptance as a guiding principle on our journey of transformation, knowing that it is the gateway to a life of fulfilment, joy, and abundance.

Chapter 4.1
Unveiling the Inner Child:
Understanding Its Needs and Wounds

As I embarked on my journey of inner healing, I found myself drawn to the concept of the inner child—a representation of the vulnerable and innocent aspects of ourselves that are often wounded by the traumas of our past. Through my own life experiences, shaped by a background of trauma and neglect, I began to unravel the layers of my inner child, seeking to understand its needs and wounds with compassion and empathy.

Growing up in a Jamaican household marked by financial struggles and emotional neglect, I learned to bury my feelings deep within myself, hiding them away in the recesses of my subconscious. Yet, despite my efforts to suppress the pain of my past, it continued to linger within me, manifesting in feelings of unworthiness, shame, and self-doubt.

As I delved deeper into the wounds of my inner child, I discovered that many of my adult struggles were rooted in experiences of abandonment and rejection from my childhood. The absence of love and nurturing from my primary caregivers left deep scars on my psyche, shaping the way I perceived myself and the world around me.

Through therapy and self-reflection, I began to uncover the unmet needs of my inner child—the need for love, acceptance, and validation that had long been denied to me. I learned to listen to the cries of my inner child with compassion and empathy, offering it the love and support it had been yearning for but never received.

Healing my inner child was not easy. It required me to confront the painful memories of my past and the ways in which they continued to influence my thoughts, feelings, and behaviours. Yet, with each step I took towards self-awareness and self-compassion, I felt a sense of liberation and empowerment that I had never known before.

Through practices such as inner child work, visualisation, and journaling, I learned to nurture and soothe my wounded inner child, offering it the love and support it needed to heal and thrive. I embraced my inner child with open arms, embracing its vulnerability and innocence and offering it the love and acceptance it had long been denied.

As I continued on my journey of inner healing, I began to see the transformative power of reconnecting with my inner child. By honouring its needs and wounds with compassion and empathy, I was able to release the grip of the past and embrace the present moment with an open heart and a renewed sense of purpose.

Today, as I reflect on my journey of healing, I am grateful for the wisdom and resilience of my inner child. It has taught me the importance of self-love and self-compassion and reminded me that healing is not a destination but a journey—a journey of self-discovery and self-empowerment that continues to unfold with each passing day.

Chapter 4.2

The Traumas of the Caregiver:

Breaking the Cycle of Suffering

In the intricate dance of caregiving, the traumas of the caregiver are often overlooked, overshadowed by the focus on the needs of those under their care. Yet, the truth remains that caregivers, too, carry their own burdens of pain and suffering, shaped by the challenges and responsibilities they face on a daily basis. As I embarked on my journey of healing, I came to understand the profound impact of caregiver trauma and the importance of breaking the cycle of suffering for both myself and my loved ones.

As a single parent navigating the complexities of parenthood, I found myself grappling with a multitude of challenges and stresses, both financial and emotional. From the relentless demands of parenting to the pressures of providing for my children on my own, the weight of responsibility often felt overwhelming. Yet, amidst the chaos and uncertainty, I also recognised the deep reservoirs of strength and resilience within myself, forged through the fires of adversity.

The traumas of the caregiver are multifaceted, encompassing not only the external pressures of parenting but also the internal struggles of managing one's own mental and emotional well-being. Research shows that caregivers, particularly women, are more likely to experience depression and anxiety as a result of the additional stress and responsibility they bear. Yet, despite the prevalence of caregiver trauma, the importance of self-care and self-compassion is often overlooked in the face of societal expectations and norms.

For me, breaking the cycle of suffering meant acknowledging the impact of caregiver trauma on my own mental and emotional health and prioritising self-care as an essential component of my healing journey. It meant carving out moments of respite amidst the chaos of daily life and seeking support from friends, family, and professionals when needed. It meant letting go of the unrealistic expectations of perfection and embracing the messy, imperfect reality of parenthood with grace and compassion.

Breaking the cycle of suffering also required me to confront the traumas of my own upbringing and the ways in which they continued to influence my thoughts, feelings, and behaviours as a parent. Through therapy and self-reflection, I learned to recognise the patterns of intergenerational trauma that had been passed down through my family and to make a conscious effort to break free from their grip.

As I continue on my journey of healing, I am reminded of the importance of breaking the cycle of suffering not only for myself but also for future generations. By addressing the traumas of the caregiver with compassion and empathy, we can create a more nurturing and supportive environment for ourselves and our loved ones, breaking free from the chains of pain and suffering that have bound us for far too long. It is only by confronting the traumas of the past and embracing the healing power of love and compassion that we can truly break free from the cycle of suffering and create a brighter, more hopeful future for ourselves and those we care for.

Steps to Healing: Recognizing and Addressing Your Inner Child's Pain

In the journey of healing, one of the most profound and transformative experiences is the recognition and addressing of our inner child's pain. Rooted in the traumas and wounds of our past, the inner child represents the vulnerable and innocent aspects of ourselves that were often neglected or abandoned during childhood. By acknowledging and addressing this pain with compassion and empathy, we can embark on a path of healing and self-discovery that leads to greater wholeness and well-being.

The first step in healing your inner child's pain is to recognise and acknowledge its existence. This requires a willingness to look inward and confront the wounds of your past, no matter how painful or uncomfortable they may be. For me, this meant facing the memories of neglect and abandonment that had haunted me for years and acknowledging the ways in which they continued to influence my thoughts, feelings, and behaviours as an adult.

Once you have recognised the presence of your inner child's pain, the next step is to cultivate a sense of compassion and empathy towards yourself. This involves treating yourself with the same kindness and understanding that you would offer to a wounded child and acknowledging that the pain you are feeling is valid and deserving of care and attention. For me, this meant learning to soothe and comfort myself in moments of distress and offering myself the love and support that I had longed for but never received.

Another important step in healing your inner child's pain is to create a safe and nurturing space for it to express itself. This may involve engaging in creative activities such as writing, drawing, journaling, or simply allowing yourself to feel and process your emotions without judgment or shame. For me, this meant setting aside time each day to connect with my inner child through journaling and meditation and allowing myself to express the pain and sadness that I had long suppressed.

As you continue on your healing journey, it is important to seek support from others who can help you navigate the complexities of your inner child's pain. This may involve seeking therapy or counselling from a trained professional, or counselling from a trained professional or connecting with friends and loved ones who can offer a listening ear and a shoulder to lean on. For me, therapy played a crucial role in my healing journey, providing me with the tools and support I needed to confront my inner child's pain and begin the process of healing.

Finally, it is important to remember that healing your inner child's pain is a process, not a destination. It may take time and patience to fully address and heal the wounds of your past, but with dedication and perseverance, it is possible to find greater wholeness and well-being. For me, the journey of healing my inner child's pain has been one of the most challenging and rewarding experiences of my life, and I am grateful for the opportunity to reclaim my sense of self and embrace the joy and freedom that comes from healing.

Chapter 5
Recognising the Signs:
When You're in Need of Healing

In the journey of healing, one of the most critical steps is recognising when you're in need of it. Often, the signs are subtle, hidden beneath the surface of our daily lives, but they manifest in our thoughts, emotions, and behaviours. By tuning into these signals and acknowledging the need for healing, we take a crucial step towards reclaiming our sense of well-being and wholeness.

One of the key indicators that you may be in need of healing is the presence of triggers—those seemingly innocuous stimuli that evoke intense emotional responses. These triggers can range from specific situations or environments to certain words or phrases, and they often stem from past traumas or unresolved wounds. For me, recognizing my triggers was a pivotal moment in my healing journey. I began to notice how certain experiences or interactions would cause me to react with anger, sadness, or fear, and I realised that these reactions were rooted in the pain of my past.

Another sign that you may be in need of healing is the presence of recurring thoughts or patterns of behaviour that are destructive or self-sabotaging. These thoughts and behaviours often stem from feelings of shame, unworthiness, or inadequacy, and they can manifest in a variety of ways—from negative self-talk and self-destructive habits to avoidance and withdrawal from others. For me, the realisation that my sudden emotional outbursts and inability to control my emotions were signs of deeper pain was a wake-up call. I knew that I needed to confront the root causes of my suffering and seek help in order to break free from these destructive patterns.

Shame is often a significant factor that prevents us from recognising our need for healing. Society's perceptions and expectations can lead us to believe that seeking help is a sign of weakness or failure, and we may feel ashamed or embarrassed to admit that we are struggling. However, it's important to remember that asking for help is a sign of strength, not weakness and that seeking support is a vital step towards healing and growth.

Acknowledging my unconscious behaviours was the first step towards my journey of self-discovery and healing. For years, I had struggled with failed relationships and a sense of inadequacy, haunted by the hurtful words of others. When someone in their anger lashed out at me, claiming I couldn't hold a man or a job, the pain cut deep, leaving scars that seemed impossible to heal.

But in that moment of darkness, I found a flicker of determination within me. I refused to let the words of others define my worth or dictate my future. I made a vow to myself that I would rise above the negativity and become the greatest version of myself.

The road ahead was not easy. I grappled with depression, battling thoughts of self-harm and despair. But through it all, my children became my guiding light, reminding me of the strength and resilience within me. I knew I had to fight for them, to show them that even in the darkest of times, there is hope.

I embarked on a journey of self-study, delving into the intricacies of counselling to better understand my own mind and emotions. I sought to unravel the mysteries of my brokenness, to uncover the root causes of my pain and suffering.

And as I navigated the depths of my own psyche, I discovered a newfound sense of clarity and purpose. The trials and tribulations I had endured were not in vain – they were stepping stones on the path to my own redemption.

Listen to me when I say this: the lower you go, the greater you will propel into the sky. Every setback, every hardship, every moment of despair serves to strengthen your resolve and propel you towards greatness.

So trust in yourself, believe in your own resilience, and never lose sight of the light within you. For even in the darkest of nights, there is always a glimmer of hope waiting to illuminate your path forward.

When I finally acknowledged that I needed help, I was met with a flood of relief and gratitude. I realized that by reaching out for support, I was taking control of my own healing journey and reclaiming my power. I refused to let societal perceptions or shame stand in the way of my well-being, and I made a commitment to prioritise my mental and emotional health above all else.

In conclusion, recognising the signs that you're in need of healing is a crucial step towards reclaiming your sense of well-being and wholeness. By tuning into your triggers, listening to your thoughts, and acknowledging the presence of shame, you can begin to break free from destructive patterns and seek the support you need to heal. Don't let societal perceptions or shame hold you back—your well-being is worth fighting for, and you deserve to live a life filled with joy, peace, and fulfilment.

Growing up as a Jamaican girl, asking for help was not something that came naturally to me. It was ingrained in me from a young age that we should be strong and self-sufficient and that asking for help was a sign of weakness. This belief was not just held by my family but by society as a whole, where phrases like "pickney fi seen and not heard" were commonly heard.

As a result, I struggled to talk about how I felt and express my emotions. I internalised the belief that I should keep my feelings to myself, which led to a buildup of emotional baggage that I carried with me into adulthood. This inability to express myself not only affected my relationships with others but also took a toll on my mental and emotional well-being.

In my intimate relationships, I found myself grappling with an anxious attachment style, characterised by a fear of abandonment and a reluctance to express my needs and emotions. I was afraid to speak up when something hurt me, fearing rejection or judgment from my partner. This pattern of behaviour led to a cycle of failed relationships, leaving me feeling even more isolated and alone.

It wasn't until I reached a breaking point, realising that I needed to change my approach if I wanted to create a healthy environment for my children, that I began to reevaluate my beliefs about asking for help. I realized that seeking support was not a sign of weakness but a sign of strength and self-awareness. I had to challenge the cultural norms that had been ingrained in me and retrain myself to ask for help when I needed it.

Breaking the silence was a decision that I had to consciously make despite the fear and discomfort that it brought. I had to learn to speak up when something hurt me, to express my needs and emotions openly and honestly, and to seek support from others when I needed it. It was a gradual process, but with each step, I felt a sense of empowerment and liberation that I had never known before.

Today, as I continue on my journey of healing, I am committed to breaking the cycle of silence and shame that has held me back for so long. I refuse to let societal expectations or cultural norms dictate how I express myself or seek help. I am determined to create a different reality for myself and for future generations, where asking for help is seen as a sign of strength and resilience, not weakness.

When you become emotionally overbearing and lack boundaries, it can have significant repercussions on your relationships and overall well-being. Without healthy boundaries in place, you may find yourself struggling to maintain respectful and balanced interactions with others, leading to strained relationships and feelings of resentment or frustration. Here are some of the consequences of being emotionally overbearing and having no boundaries:

Lack of Respect: Without boundaries, others may perceive you as overly intrusive or controlling, leading to a lack of respect for your personal space and autonomy. When you consistently overstep boundaries or disregard the boundaries of others, it can erode trust and create tension in relationships.

Inability to Say No: One of the hallmarks of healthy boundaries is the ability to assertively say no when necessary. Without boundaries, you may find yourself saying yes to requests or obligations that you don't truly want to commit to, leading to feelings of overwhelm, resentment, and burnout.

Strained Relationships: Emotionally overbearing behaviour can strain relationships with friends, family members, romantic partners, and colleagues. Constantly crossing boundaries or imposing your needs onto others can create tension and conflict, making it difficult to cultivate healthy and supportive connections.

Triggering Emotional Reactions: Lack of boundaries can contribute to heightened emotional reactivity and triggers. When others encroach upon your personal boundaries or when you struggle to assert your own boundaries, it can evoke intense emotional responses such as anger, anxiety, or sadness. These emotional reactions can further strain relationships and impede your ability to communicate effectively.

Stagnation in Personal Growth: Without boundaries, you may find yourself stuck in patterns of behaviour that perpetuate emotional overbearing tendencies. This can hinder your personal growth and prevent you from developing healthier ways of relating to yourself and others. It's essential to recognise that personal growth and transformation require self-awareness, reflection, and a willingness to establish and maintain boundaries.

To address these challenges, it's crucial to prioritise self-awareness and self-reflection. Take the time to examine your thoughts, emotions, and behaviours, paying attention to any patterns or tendencies that may indicate a lack of boundaries. Engage in practices such as mindfulness, journaling, or therapy to explore the underlying causes of your emotional overbearing tendencies and develop strategies for establishing healthier boundaries.

Remember that healing from past trauma and cultivating healthy boundaries is an ongoing process. Be patient and compassionate with yourself as you navigate this journey of self-discovery and growth. By doing the inner work to establish boundaries and respect your own needs and the needs of others, you can create more fulfilling and balanced relationships and lead a more empowered and authentic life.

Chapter 5.1

Identifying the Echoes of Neglect in Adult Behavior

Neglect, in its various forms, leaves indelible marks on the psyche of a child, often reverberating through adulthood in subtle yet profound ways. As we embark on the journey of healing, it becomes imperative to recognise and understand how the echoes of neglect manifest in our adult behaviour, shaping the way we perceive ourselves and interact with the world around us.

Neglect, a form of maltreatment, manifests in various ways, each impacting individuals differently. Here are some types of neglect:

Physical Neglect: Physical neglect occurs when a caregiver fails to provide the basic necessities for a child's physical well-being. This can include inadequate food, clothing, shelter, and healthcare. Children experiencing physical neglect may suffer from malnutrition, untreated medical conditions, or exposure to unsafe living conditions.

Emotional Neglect: Emotional neglect involves the failure to meet a child's emotional needs, such as love, affection, attention, and emotional support. Caregivers who are emotionally unavailable or dismissive of a child's feelings can contribute to emotional neglect. Children experiencing emotional neglect may struggle with low self-esteem, difficulty forming relationships, and emotional dysregulation.

Educational Neglect: Educational neglect occurs when caregivers fail to provide a child with access to education or educational support. This can include failing to enrol a child in school, allowing chronic absenteeism, or neglecting to provide necessary educational resources. Children experiencing educational neglect may fall behind academically and face barriers to future success.

Medical Neglect: Medical neglect involves the failure to provide a child with necessary medical care or treatment. This can include neglecting to seek medical attention for illness or injury, refusing to follow through with recommended medical interventions, or withholding medication or therapy. Children experiencing medical neglect may suffer from untreated medical conditions, chronic pain, or disability.

Supervisory Neglect: Supervisory neglect occurs when caregivers fail to adequately supervise and protect a child from harm. This can include leaving a child unsupervised for extended periods, exposing a child to dangerous environments or situations, or failing to intervene in instances of abuse or neglect by others. Children experiencing supervisory neglect may be at risk of accidents, injuries, or victimisation.

Moral and Religious Neglect: Moral and religious neglect involves the failure to provide a child with moral or religious guidance and instruction. This can include neglecting to instil values, morals, or beliefs in a child or preventing a child from practising their religious or spiritual beliefs. Children experiencing moral and religious neglect may struggle with issues of identity, morality, or spirituality.

It's essential to recognise that neglect can have significant and lasting effects on individuals' physical, emotional, and psychological well-being. Early intervention and support are crucial in addressing neglect and promoting the health and safety of children and families.

One of the most prevalent effects of neglect is the erosion of self-esteem. When children grow up in environments where their physical, emotional, and psychological needs are consistently unmet, they internalize the message that they are unworthy of love and attention. This deep-seated belief often carries into adulthood, manifesting as feelings of inadequacy, self-doubt, and low self-esteem.

Furthermore, neglect can hinder our ability to form healthy relationships. When we grow up without experiencing the warmth and nurturing of a loving caregiver, we may struggle to trust others and open ourselves up emotionally. This can lead to a pattern of avoidant or anxious attachment styles, characterized by a fear of intimacy and a reluctance to rely on others for support.

Educational neglect is another common form of neglect that can have lasting effects on adult behaviour. When children are deprived of access to quality education and educational support, they may struggle academically and face barriers to achieving their full potential. This can lead to feelings of frustration, inadequacy, and a lack of confidence in one's abilities.

Perhaps the most devastating consequence of neglect is the potential for experiencing sexual abuse. Children who are neglected are often more vulnerable to exploitation and victimisation, and the effects of sexual abuse can be profound and long-lasting. Survivors of sexual abuse may struggle with a range of emotional and psychological issues, including depression, anxiety, PTSD, and difficulties forming intimate relationships.

The effects of sexual abuse can be particularly devastating, often leading to profound feelings of shame, guilt, and worthlessness. Survivors may struggle to trust others, develop healthy boundaries, and experience intimacy in a safe and consensual manner. Healing from the trauma of sexual abuse requires time, support, and a commitment to reclaiming one's sense of self-worth and dignity.

In conclusion, neglect leaves a lasting imprint on the lives of those who experience it, shaping the way they perceive themselves and navigate the world around them. By recognising the echoes of neglect in our adult behaviour, we can begin to unpack the wounds of our past and embark on a journey of healing and self-discovery. Through therapy, support, and self-compassion, it is possible to break free from the chains of neglect and reclaim our sense of worth, dignity, and wholeness.

Chapter 5.2
Acknowledging the Problem:
The First Step Towards Healing

Acknowledging the presence of a problem is often the first step towards healing and transformation. When it comes to addressing deep-seated emotional wounds and patterns of behaviour, it's essential to sit down with your thoughts and confront the underlying issues head-on. This chapter explores the significance of acknowledging the problem and the importance of seeking support from counsellors or trusted individuals on your journey towards healing.

Self-Reflection and Awareness: Take the time to sit down with your thoughts and reflect on your experiences, emotions, and behaviours. Consider how your past experiences may be influencing your present relationships and interactions. Are there recurring patterns or triggers that you notice? Pay attention to your emotional reactions and physical sensations, as they can provide valuable insights into areas that may need healing.

Seeking Support from Counselors or Friends: While self-reflection is a valuable starting point, some deep-seated wounds may require the support of a counsellor or trusted friend to fully explore and address. Consider reaching out to a professional therapist or counsellor who can provide guidance, perspective, and tools for navigating your emotional landscape. Alternatively, confide in a trusted friend or loved one who can offer empathy, validation, and support as you embark on your healing journey.

Understanding Relationship Dynamics: Acknowledging the problem also involves examining your relationship dynamics, both past and present. Consider how your upbringing and early experiences with caregivers may be influencing your current relationships and communication styles. Explore your attachment patterns and love languages to gain a deeper understanding of how you relate to others emotionally. Recognise that healing begins with understanding the root causes of your emotional struggles and how they manifest in your relationships.

Recognising the Need for Professional Help: While some individuals may be able to address their emotional wounds with self-reflection and support from friends, others may benefit from the expertise of a professional counsellor or therapist. If you find that your emotional struggles are interfering with your daily life, relationships, or overall well-being, seeking professional help may be imperative to your development. A trained therapist can provide a safe and nonjudgmental space for exploring deep-seated issues and developing strategies for healing and growth.

Recognising Childhood Interpretations: The first step in healing from childhood wounds is acknowledging the interpretations and beliefs we formed as children. Reflect on the messages you received from caregivers or others who may have perpetuated emotional abuse. Consider how these messages shaped your self-image, worth, and relationships with others. Recognise that these interpretations were based on your limited understanding as a child and may not accurately reflect reality.

Distinguishing Childlike and Adult Perspectives: As adults, it is essential to distinguish between our childlike perspectives and our mature, adult perspectives. Ask yourself whether your thoughts, beliefs, and reactions are rooted in past experiences or reflect your present reality. By recognising when you are operating from a childlike frame of mind, you can begin to challenge these outdated beliefs and cultivate a more empowered, mature perspective.

Embracing Maturity and Renewal: The process of healing childhood wounds involves embracing maturity and renewal. Just as the Bible says, "When I was a child, I spoke as a child, I understood as a child, I thought as a child: but when I became a man, I put away childish things" (1 Corinthians 13:11). Embrace the opportunity to put away the limiting beliefs and behaviours associated with your childhood experiences and step into a more mature, empowered version of yourself.

Renewing Your Mind: Renewing your mind involves actively challenging and reshaping the beliefs and thought patterns that stem from childhood interpretations. Engage in practices such as mindfulness, therapy, or self-reflection to become aware of these ingrained beliefs and replace them with more empowering and accurate perspectives. Remember that healing is an ongoing process, and it takes time and effort to cultivate a renewed mind and sense of self.

Seeking Support and Guidance: Healing from childhood wounds often requires support and guidance from others. Consider seeking therapy or counselling to explore and process your experiences in a safe and supportive environment. Surround yourself with understanding and compassionate individuals who can offer validation, encouragement, and insight as you navigate your healing journey.

In conclusion, healing from childhood wounds involves embracing maturity and renewal by challenging outdated beliefs and thought patterns rooted in past experiences. By recognising when we are operating from a childlike frame of mind and actively renewing our thoughts and beliefs, we can cultivate a more empowered and mature perspective on ourselves and the world around us. Through self-awareness, self-compassion, and support from others, we can embark on a journey of healing and transformation, reclaiming our sense of self and embracing the fullness of our adult identity.

In a bustling city where skyscrapers reached for the clouds and streets buzzed with the energy of millions lived a man named Daniel. To the world, Daniel seemed to have it all – a successful career, a loving family, and a wide circle of friends. But beneath his confident exterior lay a hidden truth that he had long kept buried.

For years, Daniel had been running on autopilot, burying himself in work and filling his days with endless distractions. He was always the life of the party, the one with a quick smile and a joke on his lips.

But deep down, he carried a heavy weight that he could no longer ignore.

It wasn't until a series of life-changing events rocked Daniel's world that he finally realised he needed healing. A sudden loss in the family, followed by a painful breakup and a health scare, left him reeling and questioning everything he thought he knew about himself and his life.

In the midst of his turmoil, Daniel found himself unable to escape the nagging feeling that something was missing – that he was missing. He felt disconnected from his own emotions, as if he were merely going through the motions of life without truly experiencing it.

It was during a moment of quiet reflection that Daniel had a profound realisation – he needed to confront the pain and trauma that he had long suppressed. He needed to confront the wounds of his past in order to move forward and live a life of authenticity and wholeness.

With newfound determination, Daniel sought out therapy – a decision that would change his life forever. Through the guidance of a compassionate therapist, he began to unravel the tangled web of his past, confronting painful memories and buried emotions that he had long since pushed aside.

As he delved deeper into his own psyche, Daniel discovered layers of hurt and pain that he had long kept hidden from the world. He faced moments of intense sadness and anger as he confronted the wounds of his past, but he also discovered moments of profound healing and growth.

Through therapy, Daniel learned to embrace his vulnerability and honour the parts of himself that he had long ignored. He learned to release the shame and guilt that had held him captive for so long and to reclaim his power and his voice.

With each passing day, Daniel found himself becoming more whole – more aligned with his true self and more connected to the world around him. He learned to embrace the beauty of imperfection and to celebrate the journey of healing and self-discovery.

And though the road to healing was not always easy, Daniel knew that he was on the right path. He had finally found the courage to confront his pain and to embrace the possibility of a brighter, more fulfilling future. And as he looked ahead, Daniel knew that the best was yet to come.

Chapter 5.3

Seeking Help: Therapy and Support Networks

Seeking help is not a sign of weakness; it's a courageous step towards healing and growth. Whether it's therapy, support groups, or spiritual communities, reaching out for support can be a transformative experience on your journey towards wholeness.

Therapy, in particular, can be incredibly beneficial. It provides a safe and confidential space for you to explore your thoughts, feelings, and experiences with a trained professional. A therapist can offer valuable insights, guidance, and tools to help you navigate challenges, heal from past traumas, and cultivate a greater sense of self-awareness and resilience.

For me, going to therapy was one of the best decisions I ever made. It allowed me to confront the deep-seated wounds and patterns of behaviour that were holding me back and hindering my personal and spiritual growth. Through therapy, I gained a deeper understanding of myself and my struggles, and I learned practical strategies to cope with stress, manage my emotions, and improve my relationships.

But therapy is just one avenue of support. Support networks, such as support groups or online communities, can also play a vital role in your healing journey. Connecting with others who have shared experiences can provide validation, empathy, and encouragement and remind you that you are not alone in your struggles.

Additionally, spiritual communities can offer a unique form of support and guidance. Whether it's through prayer, meditation, or fellowship, spirituality can provide solace, strength, and a sense of purpose. For me, my faith community, Christ Liquid Fire Ministry, was instrumental in my personal and spiritual development. The love, support, and teachings I received there helped me to deepen my connection with the divine and find comfort and healing in times of need.

It's important to remember that there is no one-size-fits-all approach to seeking help. What works for one person may not work for another, and that's okay. The key is to explore different options and find what resonates with you and feels right for your unique journey.

In this book, I'll be leaving some resources for therapy and support networks that you can explore. Remember, you don't have to face your struggles alone. Help and support are available, and by reaching out, you are taking an important step towards healing, growth, and wholeness.

Societal pressures can be powerful forces, shaping our perceptions, beliefs, and behaviours in profound ways. When it comes to seeking help for our mental and emotional well-being, these pressures can often act as barriers, preventing us from reaching out and getting the support we need. But it's essential to recognise that these pressures are often based on outdated stigmas and misconceptions, and they should not dictate our decisions when it comes to our health and happiness.

One of the most pervasive societal pressures is the stigma surrounding mental health issues. For far too long, mental illness has been shrouded in secrecy and shame, with those suffering often feeling isolated and afraid to seek help. But the truth is that mental health struggles are incredibly common, affecting people from all walks of life. Seeking therapy or counselling is not a sign of weakness; it's a courageous step towards healing and self-discovery.

Another societal pressure that can hinder our ability to seek help is the expectation of self-sufficiency. We live in a culture that values independence and resilience, often to the detriment of our mental and emotional well-being. Asking for help can be seen as a sign of failure or incompetence, leading many to suffer in silence rather than reach out for support. But the reality is that we all need help from time to time, and there is strength in recognising when we need assistance and reaching out for it.

Moreover, there may be cultural or religious pressures that discourage seeking help for mental health issues. In some communities, there is a stigma attached to therapy or counselling, with mental health problems being seen as a sign of moral or spiritual weakness. But it's important to remember that mental health is just as important as physical health, and seeking help is a necessary part of taking care of ourselves.

Breaking free from these societal pressures requires courage and conviction. It means challenging the beliefs and attitudes that have been ingrained in us from a young age and forging our own path towards healing and wholeness. It means recognising that our well-being is worth prioritizing and prioritising and that seeking help is a sign of strength, not weakness.

If you find yourself hesitating to seek help because of societal pressures, I want to encourage you to take that first step. Don't let fear or shame hold you back from getting the support you need and deserve. There are people and resources available to help you on your journey towards healing, and by reaching out, you are taking an important step towards reclaiming your health, happiness, and autonomy.

In the end, what matters most is not how society perceives our choices but how we feel about ourselves and the steps we take to care for our well-being. So let go of societal pressures, embrace help and healing, and trust that you are worthy of love, support, and acceptance just as you are.

Chapter 6
Nurturing Your Inner Child

Within each of us resides an inner child—a part of ourselves that holds our deepest emotions, memories, and vulnerabilities from our formative years. This inner child is a precious aspect of our being, deserving of love, care, and attention. Nurturing your inner child is a profound act of self-compassion and healing, allowing you to reconnect with the innocence, wonder, and joy of childhood while addressing unresolved wounds and traumas.

Acknowledging Your Inner Child: The first step in nurturing your inner child is acknowledging its presence within you. Take the time to connect with this aspect of yourself, recognising its needs, fears, and desires. Reflect on your childhood experiences and how they have shaped the person you are today. By acknowledging your inner child, you create space for healing and growth to occur.

Cultivating Self-Compassion: Treat your inner child with the same kindness and compassion that you would offer to a young child. Validate its emotions and experiences, offering comfort and reassurance in times of distress. Practice self-care activities that nourish your soul and bring you joy, whether it's spending time in nature, engaging in creative expression, or simply cuddling up with a favourite book or movie.

Healing Childhood Wounds: Take the time to explore and process any unresolved wounds or traumas from your childhood.

This may involve seeking therapy or behaviour counselling to work through deep-seated issues and patterns of behaviour. Allow yourself to grieve for the pain and loss you experienced as a child, and forgive those who may have hurt you. By healing your childhood wounds, you create space for healing and transformation in your adult life.

Reparenting Yourself: Reparenting is the process of providing yourself with the love, nurturing, and guidance that you may have lacked as a child. Become your own loving parent, offering yourself the care and support that you need to thrive. Set healthy boundaries, prioritize your needs, and practice self-discipline with compassion. By reparenting yourself, you empower your inner child to heal and grow.

Embracing Playfulness and Wonder: Rediscover the magic of childhood by embracing playfulness, creativity, and wonder in your daily life. Engage in activities that ignite your imagination and spark joy, whether it's dancing in the rain, building sandcastles at the beach, or exploring new hobbies and interests. By reconnecting with your inner child's sense of wonder, you infuse your life with vitality and enthusiasm.

Living Authentically: Honor your inner child by living authentically and true to yourself. Listen to your intuition, follow your passions, and express your emotions openly and honestly. Embrace vulnerability as a strength, allowing yourself to be seen and heard without fear of judgment or rejection. By living authentically, you create a life that is aligned with your deepest values and desires.

Nurturing your inner child is a deeply healing journey that requires patience, compassion, and self-love. Affirmations and mindfulness are powerful tools that can help you reconnect with your inner child and cultivate a sense of peace and wholeness within yourself.

Start by incorporating positive affirmations into your daily routine. Speak words of kindness and encouragement to yourself, affirming your worth and value. Repeat phrases such as "I am worthy of love and happiness," "I am deserving of kindness and compassion," and "I am enough just as I am." By consistently affirming these truths, you begin to rewire your subconscious mind and shift your perspective towards one of self-acceptance and self-love.

Mindfulness practices can also play a crucial role in nurturing your inner child. Set aside time each day to quiet your mind and tune into your inner thoughts and feelings. Practice deep breathing exercises, meditation, or gentle yoga to ground yourself in the present moment and cultivate a sense of inner peace. By practising mindfulness regularly, you create space for healing and self-reflection, allowing yourself to release any pent-up emotions or negative thought patterns that may be holding you back.

Forgiveness is another essential aspect of nurturing your inner child. Holding onto resentment and anger towards those who have harmed you only serves to perpetuate your own suffering. Instead, choose to forgive those who have caused you pain, not for their sake, but for your own healing and liberation. Recognise that forgiveness is a gift you give yourself, freeing yourself from the burden of carrying around past hurts and allowing yourself to move forward with grace and compassion.

As you embark on your journey of nurturing your inner child, remember to be patient and gentle with yourself. Healing is a gradual process, and it's okay to take small steps towards self-discovery and growth. Trust in the power of affirmations, mindfulness, and forgiveness to guide you along the way, and know that you have the strength and resilience within you to overcome any obstacles that may arise.

Nurturing your inner child is a lifelong journey of self-discovery, healing, and growth. It requires patience, compassion, and a willingness to confront the shadows of the past while embracing the light of the present. By nurturing your inner child, you reclaim your innocence, reclaim your power, and reclaim your joy.

Chapter 6.1

Strategies for Self-compassion and Self-Love

Growing up without receiving love from a primary caregiver can leave deep emotional wounds that impact our ability to show compassion and love to ourselves. However, despite these challenges, it is possible to cultivate self-compassion and self-love through intentional practices and mindset shifts. This chapter explores strategies for nurturing self-compassion and self-love, even in the absence of love from a primary caregiver.

Practice Self-Kindness: Treat yourself with the same kindness and understanding that you would offer to a beloved friend or family member. When faced with self-criticism or judgmental thoughts, counter them with gentle and compassionate self-talk. Remind yourself that you are worthy of love and acceptance, regardless of past experiences.

Cultivate Mindfulness: Mindfulness involves paying attention to the present moment with openness and acceptance, without judgment. Practice mindfulness meditation or simply engage in activities that bring you into the present moment, such as deep breathing, walking in nature, or savouring a cup of tea. By cultivating mindfulness, you can become more attuned to your thoughts and emotions, allowing you to respond to yourself with greater compassion and understanding.

Challenge Negative Beliefs: Take a closer look at the negative beliefs and self-limiting thoughts that may have developed as a result of not receiving love from a primary caregiver. Challenge these beliefs by asking yourself if they are based on reality or simply remnants of past experiences. Replace negative self-talk with affirmations and positive statements that affirm your worthiness and value.

Set Boundaries: Establishing healthy boundaries is an act of self-love and self-respect. Identify your needs and priorities and communicate them assertively to others. Learn to say no to activities or relationships that drain your energy or compromise your well-being. By setting boundaries, you honour and honour your own needs and create space for self-care and self-compassion.

Seek Support: Surround yourself with supportive and understanding individuals who can offer validation, empathy, and encouragement on your journey toward self-compassion and self-love. Whether it's friends, family members, or a therapist, having a support system can provide valuable perspective and guidance as you navigate the challenges of healing from past wounds.

Practice Gratitude: Cultivate a practice of gratitude by regularly acknowledging and appreciating the positive aspects of your life. Keep a gratitude journal where you write down things you are thankful for each day, no matter how small. By focusing on the good in your life, you can shift your perspective from one of lack to one of abundance, fostering feelings of self-love and contentment.

Engage in Self-Care: Make self-care a priority in your daily life by engaging in activities that nourish your body, mind, and spirit.

This could include exercise, healthy eating, adequate sleep, creative expression, or spending time with loved ones. By prioritising self-care, you demonstrate love and compassion for yourself, nurturing your overall well-being and resilience.

Remember that self-compassion and self-love are ongoing practices that require patience, persistence, and kindness toward yourself. By implementing these strategies into your daily life, you can gradually cultivate a deeper sense of love, acceptance, and compassion for yourself, regardless of past experiences with your primary caregiver. You deserve to love and be loved, and it all starts with loving yourself.

Chapter 6.2
Building Healthy Relationships:
Learning to Trust and Love Again

After experiencing a lack of love from a primary caregiver, rebuilding trust and learning to love again can be a daunting but ultimately rewarding journey. Building healthy relationships requires intentional effort, self-awareness, and a commitment to fostering trust and security. This chapter explores strategies for cultivating trust, developing a secure attachment style, and fostering healthy, fulfilling relationships.

Understand Your Attachment Style: Take the time to understand your attachment style, which may have been influenced by your experiences with your primary caregiver. Recognise how your attachment style impacts your relationships and interactions with others. Whether you have an anxious, avoidant, or secure attachment style, awareness is the first step toward fostering healthier relational dynamics.

Practice Vulnerability: Building trust in relationships involves being willing to be vulnerable and authentic with others. Share your thoughts, feelings, and experiences openly and honestly, allowing yourself to be seen and accepted for who you are. Embrace vulnerability as a strength rather than a weakness, knowing that it is essential for building deep and meaningful connections with others.

Set Healthy Boundaries: Establishing and maintaining healthy boundaries is crucial for fostering trust and mutual respect in relationships. Clearly communicate your needs, preferences, and limits to others, and be assertive in enforcing them. Respect the boundaries of others as well, recognising that boundaries are essential for creating a safe and supportive relational environment.

Take Things Slowly: Avoid rushing into relationships or placing undue pressure on yourself or others to progress quickly. Take the time to get to know someone gradually, allowing trust and intimacy to develop naturally over time. Focus on building a foundation of friendship, mutual respect, and shared values before diving into deeper levels of emotional intimacy.

Communicate Effectively: Open and honest communication is essential for building trust and resolving conflicts in relationships. Practice active listening, empathy, and assertive communication skills to ensure that your needs and concerns are heard and understood. Be willing to express your feelings and address issues as they arise rather than sweeping them under the rug.

Give and Receive Love: Learning to trust and love again also involves being open to giving and receiving love freely. Allow yourself to experience love in all its forms, whether from romantic partners, friends, or family members. Be willing to show affection, express gratitude, and offer support to others, knowing that love is a fundamental human need that enriches our lives.

Seek Support and Guidance: Don't hesitate to seek support and guidance from trusted friends, family members, or a therapist as you navigate the challenges of rebuilding trust and fostering healthy relationships. A supportive network can offer valuable perspective, encouragement, and accountability as you work toward healing and growth.

In conclusion, building healthy relationships after experiencing a lack of love from a primary caregiver requires patience, self-awareness, and a willingness to learn and grow. By understanding your attachment style, practising vulnerability, setting healthy boundaries, and communicating effectively, you can foster trust, intimacy, and mutual respect in your relationships. Remember that healing is a journey, and each step you take toward building healthier relationships brings you closer to experiencing the love and connection you deserve.

Chapter 6.3
Establishing Boundaries:
Protecting Your Emotional Well-Being

Establishing boundaries is crucial for protecting your emotional well-being and fostering healthy relationships. For individuals with anxious attachment styles, setting boundaries may be particularly challenging, as they may struggle to assert their needs and express themselves authentically. Additionally, the relationship with food can be intertwined with emotional boundaries, impacting one's overall well-being. This chapter explores the importance of establishing boundaries and strategies for protecting your emotional well-being, particularly for those with anxious attachment styles and concerning their relationship with food.

Understanding Anxious Attachment Styles: Individuals with anxious attachment styles often fear rejection or abandonment and may seek excessive reassurance and closeness in relationships. As a result, they may struggle to set healthy boundaries and assert their needs, leading to feelings of insecurity and emotional turmoil. Recognise the impact of your attachment style on your ability to establish boundaries and prioritise your emotional well-being.

Identifying Your Needs and Limits: Take the time to identify your needs, preferences, and limits in various areas of your life, including relationships, work, and self-care. Reflect on situations where you may have felt uncomfortable or overwhelmed due to a lack of boundaries, and consider what boundaries you can implement to protect your emotional well-being. Remember that setting boundaries is an act of self-care and self-respect.

Communicating Boundaries Assertively: Practice assertive communication skills to effectively communicate your boundaries to others. Clearly express your needs, preferences, and limits in a respectful and assertive manner without apologizing for apologising or feeling guilty for prioritising your well-being. Use "I" statements to express how certain behaviours or situations impact you personally, and be open to negotiating compromises when necessary.

Recognizing Boundary Violations: Be vigilant in recognising and addressing boundary violations in your relationships and interactions with others. Pay attention to situations where your boundaries are disregarded or ignored, and assertively communicate your discomfort or dissatisfaction. Trust your instincts and prioritise your emotional well-being, even if it means confronting difficult situations or setting firmer boundaries.

Developing Self-Compassion: Cultivate self-compassion and self-kindness as you navigate the process of establishing boundaries. Understand that setting boundaries may feel uncomfortable or challenging at times, especially if you have a history of anxious attachment or people-pleasing tendencies. Be patient and gentle with yourself, and acknowledge the courage and resilience it takes to prioritise your emotional well-being.

Exploring Your Relationship with Food: Recognise the potential connection between your relationship with food and your emotional boundaries. For some individuals, food may serve as a coping mechanism for managing difficult emotions or soothing anxiety. Reflect on your relationship with food and consider how setting boundaries around eating habits, meal times, and food choices can support your overall well-being.

Seeking Support and Guidance: Don't hesitate to seek support and guidance from trusted friends, family members, or a therapist as you work on establishing boundaries and protecting your emotional well-being. A supportive network can offer validation, encouragement, and accountability as you navigate the challenges of setting boundaries and fostering healthier relationships.

In conclusion, establishing boundaries is essential for protecting your emotional well-being and fostering healthy relationships. For individuals with anxious attachment styles, setting boundaries may require extra care and attention, but it is an important aspect of self-care and self-respect. By identifying your needs, communicating assertively, and prioritising your emotional well-being, you can create a safe and supportive environment that honours your boundaries and nurtures your overall well-being, including your relationship with food.

Chapter 7
Forgiving and Moving Forward

Forgiveness is a powerful act of liberation that allows us to release the weight of past hurts and embrace a future filled with peace and healing. In this chapter, we will explore the transformative journey of forgiveness, acknowledging the role of generational trauma and understanding that our parents themselves may have been carrying their own wounds.

Acknowledging Generational Trauma: Recognise that the wounds you carry may not only stem from your own experiences but also from generational trauma passed down through your family lineage. Just as you have been impacted by your parents' traumas, they too may have inherited their pain from previous generations. Understanding this can help foster empathy and compassion as you navigate the process of forgiveness.

Empathising with Your Parents: Take a moment to empathise with your parents and acknowledge the struggles they may have faced in their own lives. Consider the challenges and traumas they may have encountered and how these experiences may have shaped their behaviours, behaviours and parenting styles. Remember that they are human beings with their own vulnerabilities and limitations.

Reflecting on Your Own Growth: Reflect on your own journey of growth and healing and the ways in which you have been able to break free from the cycle of generational trauma. Celebrate your resilience and strength in overcoming adversity, and recognise the progress you have made in forging a path of healing for yourself and future generations.

Choosing Forgiveness: Make the conscious choice to forgive your parents for any pain they may have caused you, whether intentionally or unintentionally. Understand that forgiveness is not about excusing or condoning harmful behaviour but rather about releasing yourself from the burden of resentment and anger. By choosing forgiveness, you reclaim your power and pave the way for healing and reconciliation.

Releasing Resentment: Practice letting go of resentment and bitterness towards your parents, recognising that holding onto these negative emotions only perpetuates your own suffering. Allow yourself to experience the emotions that arise as you process past hurts, but ultimately choose to release them with compassion and understanding.

Setting Healthy Boundaries: As you forgive and move forward, it is important to set healthy boundaries in your relationship with your parents. Establish clear expectations for how you wish to be treated and communicate these boundaries assertively and respectfully. Remember that boundaries are essential for maintaining your emotional well-being and fostering healthy relationships.

Seeking Support: Don't hesitate to seek support from trusted friends, family members, or a therapist as you navigate the journey of forgiveness and moving forward. Talking to others who can offer empathy, validation, and guidance can provide valuable perspective and support as you work through complex emotions and experiences.

In conclusion, forgiveness is a transformative journey that allows us to break free from the cycle of generational trauma and embrace a future filled with healing and possibility. By acknowledging the humanity of our parents, empathising with their struggles, and choosing forgiveness, we reclaim our power and pave the way for a brighter, more compassionate future. As we release resentment and set healthy boundaries, we create space for healing, reconciliation, and the possibility of building deeper, more authentic connections with ourselves and others.

In some families, dealing with a narcissistic parent can be an incredibly challenging and emotionally taxing experience. These parents often exhibit a pattern of behaviour characterised by self-centeredness, manipulation, and a lack of empathy for others, including their own children. When confronted with their actions or confronted with the need for accountability, narcissistic parents may refuse to take responsibility and instead shift blame onto their children.

For individuals who have grown up with narcissistic parents, seeking closure or acknowledgement of wrongdoing may be an elusive goal. These parents may never offer a genuine apology or take accountability for their actions, leaving their children feeling invalidated and unsupported. In such cases, it is essential for individuals to come to terms with the reality that closure may never be attainable from their narcissistic parent.

Accepting the lack of closure from a narcissistic parent can be a difficult but necessary step towards healing and moving forward. It involves acknowledging the limitations of the relationship and accepting that the parent may never change their behaviour or provide the validation and acknowledgement desired by their child.

Instead of waiting for closure from a narcissistic parent, individuals can focus on their own healing and well-being. This may involve setting boundaries to protect themselves from further emotional harm, seeking support from trusted friends or therapists, and cultivating self-compassion and self-validation.

Finding closure within oneself, rather than seeking it externally from a narcissistic parent, can be empowering and liberating. It involves recognising one's own worth and value independent of external validation and embracing the journey of self-discovery and self-acceptance.

While the lack of closure from a narcissistic parent may be painful, it is important for individuals to remember that their worth and identity are not defined by their parent's actions or lack thereof. By prioritising their own emotional well-being and cultivating self-love and self-compassion, individuals can begin to heal from the wounds inflicted by their narcissistic parents and create a brighter, more fulfilling future for themselves.

Chapter 7.2
Reconciling with the Past:
Understanding but Not Excusing

In the journey of personal growth and healing, confronting the past is often an inevitable step. However, this process is not about excusing or justifying past actions but rather about understanding them and their impact on our lives. Reconciliation with the past requires a delicate balance between acknowledging the pain it has caused and recognising the humanity within ourselves and others.

Understanding the Root Causes

To reconcile with the past, it's essential to delve into the root causes of our experiences. This involves exploring the circumstances, traumas, and influences that shaped our behaviours and choices. By gaining insight into our past, we can begin to unravel the complex web of emotions and beliefs that may be holding us back.

Acceptance and Forgiveness

Acceptance is a crucial aspect of reconciliation, allowing us to come to terms with our past and its consequences. It involves acknowledging the truth of what has happened without judgment or resistance. From this place of acceptance, we can then move towards forgiveness – not for the sake of those who have wronged us, but for our own healing and liberation.

Setting Boundaries

While reconciliation involves understanding and forgiveness, it also requires setting boundaries to protect ourselves from further harm. Boundaries are essential for establishing healthy relationships and maintaining our emotional well-being. By clearly defining our limits and communicating them assertively, we can create space for healing and growth while honouring our own needs and boundaries.

Cultivating Compassion

Reconciliation with the past also involves cultivating compassion – both for ourselves and for others. It requires seeing ourselves and those who have hurt us with empathy and understanding, recognising the humanity and inherent worth within each of us. Through compassion, we can transcend feelings of anger, resentment, and bitterness and move towards a place of peace and acceptance.

Moving Forward with Purpose

Ultimately, reconciliation with the past is about finding meaning and purpose in our experiences. It's about embracing the lessons learned and using them as catalysts for growth and transformation. By integrating our past into our present, we can chart a course for a brighter future, one defined by resilience, courage, and authenticity.

In conclusion, reconciling with the past is a deeply personal and transformative journey. It requires courage, compassion, and a willingness to confront the truths that lie within us. By understanding but not excusing our past, we can pave the way for healing, forgiveness, and, ultimately, liberation.

This chapter emphasises the importance of reconciling with the past while acknowledging its complexities and challenges. It encourages readers to approach this process with compassion, acceptance, and a commitment to personal growth. If you'd like to focus on any specific aspect or add more depth to certain themes, feel free to let me know!

Chapter 7.3
Building a New Legacy:
The Choice of Love Over Resentment

In the journey of healing and reconciliation, one of the most powerful choices we can make is to build a new legacy founded on love and compassion rather than allowing resentment to dictate our relationships and behaviours. In this chapter, we delve into the transformative power of forgiveness and the importance of fostering healthy connections as we navigate the path towards healing.

The Imperative of Forgiveness: Forgiveness is not just an act of compassion towards others; it is also an essential component of our own healing journey. By choosing to forgive those who have caused us pain and hurt, we release the burden of resentment and open ourselves up to the possibility of healing and growth. Forgiveness does not mean condoning or excusing harmful behaviour; rather, it is a conscious decision to let go of the past and reclaim our power to create a better future.

Letting Go of Pain and Hurt: Holding onto resentment only perpetuates our own suffering and keeps us trapped in a cycle of negativity. When we choose to let go of pain and hurt, we free ourselves from the chains of the past and create space for healing and transformation. This requires courage and vulnerability as we confront our own pain and acknowledge the ways in which it has impacted our lives.

Focusing on Healthy Connections: As we release resentment and embrace forgiveness, we can begin to cultivate healthy connections with others based on mutual respect, empathy, and understanding. Surrounding ourselves with supportive and nurturing relationships is essential for our emotional well-being and allows us to experience love and connection in its truest form. By prioritising healthy connections, we create a supportive network of individuals who uplift and empower us on our journey of healing.

Choosing Love Over Resentment: Ultimately, the choice to build a new legacy founded on love over resentment is ours to make. It requires us to let go of old wounds and embrace the possibility of a brighter future filled with compassion, kindness, and understanding. This choice is not always easy, and it may require us to confront uncomfortable emotions and face difficult truths. However, the rewards of choosing love over resentment are immeasurable as we experience the freedom and joy that come from living with an open heart and a spirit of forgiveness.

In conclusion, building a new legacy founded on love over resentment is a transformative journey that requires courage, compassion, and a willingness to let go of the past. By embracing forgiveness, letting go of pain and hurt, and focusing on healthy connections, we can create a future filled with love, healing, and possibility. As we continue on this journey, may we remember that the power to build a new legacy lies within each of us and that through our choices and actions, we can create a world where love reigns supreme.

In the journey of healing from trauma, there comes a pivotal moment where surrender becomes not just an option but a necessity. It's a surrender that transcends mere resignation; it's a profound letting go, an acknowledgement that there is a higher power at work, orchestrating the intricate symphony of our lives.

For many, this higher power is found in the divine presence of God. Surrendering to God means releasing the burden of pain, hurt, and anguish that weighs heavy on the soul. It means acknowledging that there are aspects of our wounds that are beyond our own capacity to heal and entrusting them to the care of a loving and all-knowing Creator.

Surrendering to God is an act of faith, a recognition that there is a purpose to our suffering, even if we cannot see it in the midst of our pain. It requires humility, vulnerability, and a willingness to let go of the need to control every aspect of our lives. In surrender, we find solace, strength, and the beginnings of true healing.

One of the most profound aspects of surrendering to God is entrusting our loved ones to His care. For parents, this can be an especially challenging journey. We want to protect our children from harm, to shield them from the harsh realities of the world. But in surrendering our children to God, we acknowledge that His love and protection far surpass our own.

Trusting God with our children means relinquishing our fears and anxieties about their future. It means recognising that, ultimately, they are not ours to control but God's precious creations entrusted to our care for a time. It means praying fervently for their well-being while also having faith that God's plans for them far exceed anything we could ever imagine.

I remember the moments when I would pray, pouring out my heart to God, asking Him to be the father figure my children never had. And in those moments of surrender, I felt a peace wash over me, knowing that God was indeed filling the void in their lives with His boundless love and wisdom.

Surrendering to God does not mean passivity or resignation. It is an active process of faith, hope, and trust. It is choosing to believe that, even in the darkest of times, God is working all things together for our good. It is finding strength in surrender and allowing God to do the transformative work of healing in our lives.

As we surrender our pain, our fears, and our loved ones to God, we open ourselves up to a deeper experience of His grace and mercy. We allow His light to penetrate the darkest corners of our souls, bringing healing, restoration, and, ultimately, peace. In the embrace of divine surrender, we find the courage to face our wounds, knowing that we are never alone and that God is always with us, guiding us and carrying us through every trial and tribulation.

A Prayer for the person reading this book.

Dear Lord,

We humbly come before you with open hearts, seeking your guidance and strength. Bless every soul reading these words with the power to overcome the trials of trauma. Grant them resilience to rise above challenges, finding healing and restoration in your boundless love.

Illuminate the path of every child and parent, guiding them to be their best selves. Shower them with wisdom, patience, and compassion as they navigate life's journey together. May love flourish in their hearts, fostering understanding, empathy, and unity in their relationships.

May your divine light shine upon all who seek solace and empowerment, leading them to peace, fulfilment, and abundant blessings. In your name, we pray. Amen.